New Enlarged 1

Between
You and I

A LITTLE BOOK OF *BAD* ENGLISH
by James Cochrane

Introduced by John Humphrys

Includes George Orwell's famous essay
'Politics and the English Language'

Icon Books

This edition published in the UK in 2004 by Icon Books Ltd,
The Old Dairy, Brook Road, Thriplow, Cambridge SG8 7RG
e-mail: info@iconbooks.co.uk
www.iconbooks.co.uk

Original edition published in 2003
Reprinted 2003 (twice), 2004

Sold in the UK, Europe, South Africa and Asia
by Faber and Faber Ltd, 3 Queen Square,
London WC1N 3AU
or their agents

Distributed in the UK, Europe, South Africa and Asia
by TBS Ltd, Frating Distribution Centre, Colchester Road,
Frating Green, Colchester CO7 7DW

This edition published in Australia in 2004
by Allen & Unwin Pty. Ltd,
PO Box 8500, 83 Alexander Street,
Crows Nest, NSW 2065

Distributed in Canada by
Penguin Books Canada,
10 Alcorn Avenue, Suite 300,
Toronto, Ontario M4V 3B2

ISBN 1 84046 605 7

Typesetting by Hands Fotoset

Printed and bound in the UK by
Mackays of Chatham

Contents

Author's Preface to the Second Edition

Between You and I is a book about Bad English. It is not about four-letter words or slang or split infinitives or ending a sentence with a preposition. Even less is it about U and non-U. It is not written from any inclination to be purist in the sense of proposing that change is to be resisted at all costs; on the contrary, not only is change inevitable but the constant renewal and enlargement of our wonderful language is generally to be welcomed rather than not. The kind of Bad English I was concerned with in compiling it is rarely to be found either in well-educated or in uneducated speech and writing, both of which have their strengths and weaknesses. It is a particular form of debasement which derives at least in part from what might be called the 'half-educated' use of the language.

Many of the words and phrases I included are, like the phrase that gives the book its title, spoken and written by people in the belief that they are more 'correct' than the English they would have spoken naturally. Others are expressions from learned or technical discourse, often Latin or Greek by derivation, used – at best unnecessarily, at worst wrongly – in preference to humbler, common-or-garden expressions with the same meaning: 'epicentre', 'criteria' and 'discrete' spring to mind as examples. Others still are clichés used mindlessly; Simon Hoggart, in his review of the first edition of *Between You and I*, quoted the health minister who told the House of Commons: 'We are rolling out fresh fruit in primary schools.'

Almost invariably the examples come from people who ought to know better: broadcasters, particularly on BBC Radios 3 and 4, journalists on the 'quality' newspapers, politicians, public figures of all kinds and, sadly, many teachers in both schools and universities, victims themselves, perhaps, of primary education in the 'progressive' 1960s and 70s.

Fortunately, this can be a 'Little Book', because the commonest examples of this kind of Bad English are still relatively few. As a result it can be read in only an hour or two. During that time, many readers may be surprised to find that much of what they thought was 'bad' English is in fact perfectly good, and that what they have been led to think of as 'good' English is sometimes ignorant, dishonest or plain stupid.

The first edition of *Between You and I* aroused the ire of Professor Terry Eagleton, who reviewed it in the *Irish Times* and hesitated for some time before deciding that the author was not a 'quasi-fascist' but 'just an old-fashioned English snob'. (I'm actually an old-fashioned Scot; whether I'm also a snob I leave it to the reader to decide). Other reviewers were much kinder, and many readers took the trouble to write to say how much they had enjoyed the book and how grateful they were to see so many of their own favourite bugbears denounced in print. Most of them, unlike the sternly Marxist Professor Eagleton, also managed to recognise a vein of humour running through the book. I am grateful to them for their kind words and for their suggestions about possible additional entries, some of which they will find in the pages that follow.

James Cochrane, May 2004

The story is told in journalistic circles of a crowd of journalists gathered outside the house of a very important man, all of them waiting for a very important announcement. The great man's butler came to the door, drew breath and bellowed: 'Would the press go around to the tradesman's entrance and will the gentleman from *The Times* please come with me!'

Ah, those were the days: the days when *The Times* was not just a newspaper but an institution. Pompous, stuffy and old-fashioned it might have been, but it was respected throughout the world for its high standards. It was the newspaper of record. When *The Times* spoke, the world took note. It got things right.

So when, a few years ago, I was asked to write my first column for *The Times*, I was flattered and agreed immediately. On the morning of publication I opened my copy. The headline above one of the stories on my page read: 'Work Comes Second For

Tony And I'. In case you did not know, newspaper headlines are written not by the contributors but by sub-editors.

I was shocked. That a sub on *The Times* should commit such a howler was beyond belief. It was time, perhaps, to give up and accept that the battle for good English had been lost. It was all over. But then the letters began to arrive: a trickle that became a torrent. The readers were as shocked as I had been. And that reassured me. There are still many people out there who care enough for the English language to register their protest when they see it being desecrated. Many battles have been lost, but the war is not yet over.

Perhaps it should be. Perhaps those of us who recoil at the incorrect use of 'I' in a great newspaper are pedants. There is, after all, a danger that if we old fogies have our way the language will be treated as though it were a precious artefact in a museum. It will be kept carefully guarded day and night, protected from potential vandals. No one must be allowed to touch.

The French are a bit like that. The French Academy is the unchallengeable authority. It issues edicts about what may and may not be said and written. It strives to purge the sacred French language of any foreign – especially English – words that might defile its purity. It fails – and so it should.

Like any other organism, language changes. It lives in the real world and gets knocked about from time to time. It adapts in order to survive. Look up almost any word in the *Oxford English Dictionary* and you can follow the journey that it has taken over the centuries, changing its precise meaning as it twists and turns with the passing of time. Often its present meaning bears little relationship to its original one. It is silly to imagine that this evolution can be halted. It is even sillier to try.

But that is different from hoisting the white flag and surrendering to linguistic anarchy. A degree of discipline is not a constraint; it is a liberation. The more clearly we are able to express ourselves, the less room there is for ambiguity. The more elaborate and the more precise our vocabulary, the greater the scope for thought and expression. Language is about subtlety and nuance. It is powerful and it is potent. We can woo with words and we can wound. Despots fear the words of the articulate opponent. Successful revolutions are achieved with words as much as with weapons.

That is why Big Brother in George Orwell's *Nineteen Eighty-four* had teams of workers endlessly removing words from the dictionary. Ultimately there would be no free expression, no way to express dissent. Utter obedience to totalitarian authority would be the only option.

When words with wholly distinct meanings become synonymous with each other – flaunt and flout, for instance – we begin to lose the capacity for discriminated expression. When we are cavalier about where we place the word 'only' in a sentence we risk destroying its meaning. James Cochrane nicely illustrates that with his comic quotation from Marghanita Laski.

All this matters more in written than in spoken English. I have always felt it a little unfair for parliamentary sketch writers to mock John Prescott by reproducing his garbled sentences verbatim in print. It might be difficult to follow him on the page, but he is capable of making a powerful speech. His audiences may not follow every point in his argument, but they know exactly what he means. I once saw him sway an audience at a Labour Party conference and win a crucially important vote that had been thought lost. He spoke from the heart and not the head and there is nothing wrong with that. But the writer does not have that licence.

Flowery language from the pen of a poet is one thing; written English as a means of everyday communication is another. It should be plain and simple and accurate. It should use no more words than are needed to do the job and they should be the right words. We all have our own pet hates. One of mine is the relatively recent and altogether hideous American import 'met up with'. I have offered a bottle of the best bubbly to anyone who can explain how that differs from 'met'. The bottle sits in my office to this day. I am with our post-war prime minister, Clement Attlee, on this. It was said of him that he would never use one word when none would do.

Then there is the tendency to use nouns as verbs. 'Impact' is a good (by which I mean bad) example. Sadly, it has now entered the category of James Cochrane's 'Lost Causes'. They keep coming.

'Fast track' was bad enough when it was over-used as a noun. It is unspeakable as a verb.

This sort of thing flattens the language and destroys its vitality. 'Disinterested' is an excellent word with a precise meaning. Now that it is used interchangeably with 'uninterested' by those who should know better, its meaning has been destroyed. It is sad to lose a good word.

This is all of a piece with our lazy acceptance of jargon, using words for merely instrumental purposes rather than for genuine expression. It is not new. Orwell made the point in his classic essay 'Politics and the English Language' (see page 127). Political speeches, he said, 'consist less and less of words chosen for the sake of their meaning and more of phrases tacked together like the sections of a prefabricated hen-house.'

Politicians have a lot to answer for, but the real villains are business people. Management speak has been infiltrated into our lives, a loathsome serpent crawling into our bed at night and choking the life out of our language. It is an outrage that the phrase 'human resources' was not strangled at birth. I hate it for its ugliness and its sloppiness. A moment's thought tells you that 'resources' are exploited, used up, squeezed for every last drop of value and then replaced. Are we really meant to regard human beings in that light? It seems we are. Or perhaps the vandals who created the phrase think that shortening it to 'HR' erases the guilt. It does not.

Less offensive, but equally dreary, is all the mumbo-jumbo surrounding 'delivering objectives' by 'thinking outside the box' or 'stretching the envelope' by 'building on best practice'. What does it all mean? I doubt that anyone really knows, least of all the people who use it. They tend to be middle managers striving to impress their bosses or, possibly, each other. The people at the top, in my experience, tend to communicate clearly. Maybe that's why they made it to the top in the first place. Lazy use of language suggests lazy thinking.

This hen-house language might not matter if it were confined to the business world. But it has escaped, like some malign virus, and is infecting us all. I would love to claim that the BBC, with its proud history of championing good English, is fighting back. Sadly, it is not. We have been suborned. A colleague of mine interviewed a young man who was applying for a job in his department. He asked him what he had been doing in the few months since he left Cambridge. He was told: 'Proactively networking.'

He should have had him thrown out of the building on the spot or, better still, publicly executed, his body left to hang in the lobby of Television Centre as a warning to others. Instead he gave him the job. The young man is now, I have no doubt, a middle manager telling his colleagues how he can 'progress' his latest challenge – or some such rubbish.

There are so many threats to the survival of good, plain English that it is not easy to be optimistic. E-mail has a great deal to answer for. Punctuation is no longer required and verbs are abandoned with the speed of a striptease artiste late for her next performance. Text messaging is worse – much worse. Yet I have seen it suggested that students be allowed to use 'texting' abbreviations in examinations. Ultimately, no doubt, we shall communicate with a series of grunts – and the evolutionary wheel will have turned full circle.

Happily, there are people like James Cochrane still prepared to fight the good fight. His subtitle is 'A little book of bad English'. There is a lot in it for a little book. Mr Cochrane acknowledges that English is a living language and must change. But it must also be protected. We will all recognise many of his examples and have many more of our own. There is infinite scope for an infinite number of future editions.

John Humphrys, 2003

abrogate, arrogate   A letter about the international war crimes tribunal in the *Guardian* on 11 April 2003 stated that powerful nations had '*abrogated* to themselves the decision as to whether or not to recognise it' (italics added). Four days later, to its credit, the *Guardian* printed a correction: the word should have been *arrogated*.

To *abrogate* is to cancel, repeal, revoke.

To *arrogate* is to lay claim to something (normally an authority, a right, a position) without justification. The adjective is *arrogant*.

adverse, averse   These two words are easily confused but should not be. *Adverse* means 'unfavourable', 'hostile', 'harmful', as in '*adverse* weather conditions', 'an *adverse* reaction', '*adverse* effects'.

Averse can refer only to the inclinations of a person and means 'disinclined', 'reluctant'. It stems from Latin words meaning 'turned from', and for

11

that reason it was once correct English to say *averse from*; *averse to* is now much more usual.

agenda   'Today's *agenda* is dauntingly long.'

This looks at first sight like a Lost Cause. *Agenda* used to be a Latin gerundive plural, meaning 'things requiring to be done', and on the face of it should be followed by a plural verb. But since no one nowadays admits to having only a singular *agendum* and since *agenda* has come to mean 'a list of things requiring to be done or discussed' it is not really surprising that *agenda* has become a singular noun whose plural is *agendas*.

But see also REFERENDUM.

alibi   Properly used, this is a legal term for a plea that when a crime was committed the accused was somewhere else, *alibi* being a Latin word meaning 'elsewhere'. The word is often used as if it meant simply 'an excuse, a pretext' but should not be.

alternate, alternative   *Alternate* can be a verb or an adjective conveying the idea of two things being done by turns, as in 'the special service takes

12

place on *alternate* Tuesdays' or 'to build the wall he used layers of brick *alternated* with flint and mortar'.

Alternative originally meant 'the other of two' but it is now perfectly acceptable for it to mean a choice from among two or more things, courses of action etc. Since the 1960s it has been used to mean 'other than the traditional or the orthodox', as in '*alternative* medicine' or 'the *alternative* society'.

In the US especially, *alternate* is often found where standard British English would use *alternative*; for example as an adjective – the Book of the Month Club offers '*alternate* selections' – or as a noun for a reserve in sport or a reserve juror. However, it is normally a mistake in British English to write *alternate* or *alternately* where *alternative* or *alternatively* is intended.

amount, number   *Amount* should normally be used with nouns which have no plural: for example *confusion, flattery, money, timber*, whereas *number* is used with countable nouns, or in other words nouns which have plurals: for example *children, weapons, problems, bills*. The use of *amount* where *number* would normally be used is acceptable if the plural noun that follows is viewed as an aggregate, as in 'She noticed the amount of peas he was piling on his plate', where the peas are seen as a pile rather than actually counted, but too often it is used in this way with no justification whatsoever.

See also LESS AND FEWER.

apostrophe, greengrocer's   The term is used to describe the practice of forming the plural of a noun by the addition of an *apostrophe* followed by *s*, as in *potato's*, *banana's* etc. This is a little unfair to greengrocers, since they are by no means the only culprits, and the practice has spread to trades and even professions whose practitioners certainly ought to know better, for example journalists, lawyers and estate agents.

The apostrophe is correctly used to express the possessive form of a noun ('the cat's whiskers') or to indicate that a letter has been omitted in a contraction such as 'don't', 'haven't', 'isn't' etc. But note that pronouns do not need an apostrophe in their possessive form; hence the possessive form of *it* is *its*; the contracted form of *it is* is *it's*.

An apostrophe followed by *s* should be used for

the possessive case in personal names except in cases where the resulting sound is unacceptably odd because, for example, there is an internal *s* in a name also ending with that letter; hence *Lucy's*, *James's*, *Dickens's*, but *Moses'*, *Ulysses'*, *Jesus'*.

Since most plurals end with an *s*, no further *s* is added to form the possessive, hence 'the neighbours' children', 'a cats' chorus'. Where a plural noun is formed other than by adding an *s* – for example: *children*, *men* – an *s* is added, and the correct possessive form is, for example, *children's* and *men's*. But the placing of the apostrophe in such words seems to be beyond the competence of many, even those who ought to know better, such as undergraduates of a certain Cambridge college, who were recently observed sporting rowing shirts emblazoned with 'Magdalene Boat Club *Mens'* Novice Squad 2002'.

as and like   Nowadays so many people say 'It looks *like* it's going to rain' rather than 'It looks *as if* it's going to rain' that this must probably be deemed a Lost Cause. It is also unlikely that people are going to be persuaded to give up 'It feels *like* I'm falling in love' in favour of 'It feels *as if* I'm falling in love'. However, the distinction between *like* and *as* is worth preserving in the name of both clarity and common sense.

Consider the following sentences:

'*Like* tape recorders, people can now use this machine to copy CDs for little more than the cost of a blank disk.' (Heard on BBC Radio 4)

'*Like* all journeys in this country, it is almost impossible to travel anywhere with any confidence that you will arrive within a day of your anticipated time.' (Jeremy Paxman in the *Spectator*, 9 November 2002)

'*Like* 1991, most of the people of Basra are hoping for liberation from the regime in Baghdad.' (BBC Radio 4 reporter during the war in Iraq)

In the case of the first of these sentences, it should be evident that 'people' are not '*like* tape recorders' and that the speaker should have said '*As* with tape recorders'. In the same way, Jeremy Paxman would have done better to write, '*As* with all journeys in this country', and the BBC reporter on Iraq to have said, '*As* in 1991 ...'.

The mistaken usage sometimes goes in the

opposite direction, as in this example from BBC Radio 3: '*As* my other selections this morning, this 2CD album is available at mid-price', where it would have been logical as well as correct to say, '*Like* my other selections'.

The grammatical rule is that *like* should be used before nouns (including personal names), noun phrases and pronouns and *as* should be used before adverbs and prepositions ('*as* previously', '*as* in', '*as* with' etc.), but it is important also to be clear about what is being compared with what, as for example in the case of '*like* tape recorders' above.

as far as ... If we choose to start with this form of words it is necessary to complete it at some point by saying ... *is/are concerned*, as in '*As far as* my own opinions on the matter *are concerned* ...' or simply ... *goes*, as in '*As far as* that *goes*'. To say something like '*as far as* United's chances this season, I'm not holding my breath' is lazy and uneducated.

bacterium   This is the singular form. *Bacteria* is the plural, but is so often used as a singular noun even in broadsheet newspapers that it is in danger of becoming a Lost Cause. The distinction seems worth preserving, if only in serious medical and scientific discourse.

basis, on a ...   It can hardly ever be necessary to use this formula – as in *on a daily basis* or *on a regular basis*, rather than simply *daily* or *regularly* – unless it is to make a mock of a particular kind of pompous or bureaucratic discourse.

begging the question   This is a term in logic denoting an allegation based on a premiss which has not been proved and which therefore *begs the question*: what is the evidence for that claim you slipped into what you've just said? An example might be: 'Cows must be more intelligent than cats because their heads are bigger', which makes an assumption that *begs* to be challenged: namely that intelligence is directly linked to head size.

The phrase *begs the question* is occasionally used correctly in this way, but much more often it is used as if it meant simply *raises*, or *leads to*, a question, as in 'Duffy's performance in last Saturday's game *begs the question* how much longer he can remain in the England squad'. In this sentence, *raises the question* would have conveyed the speaker's meaning perfectly well, without devaluing a useful, if rather technical expression.

behalf of, on This phrase means, or should mean, either 'in the interest or for the benefit of' or 'as the agent, spokesman or representative of', as in 'I want to thank you *on behalf of* the whole family'. It is a serious mistake to use it in place of *on the part of* or to use *behalf* as a substitute for *part*, as in 'That was a bad move *on your behalf*'.

between ... to This is an odd and infuriating use of the word *between*, which is normally and correctly used to signify a distinction or a difference, an interval between two points or a relationship between two parties: we talk of the distance *between* London *and* Birmingham or the friendship *between* David *and* Jonathan. We talk about the difference *between* chalk *and* cheese.

In other words, when we are talking about two different things or points or parties *between* is invariably followed by *and*. Yet how often do we hear a weather forecaster talk of 'temperatures *between* 20 *to* 25 degrees' or see notices announcing that 'opening hours are *between* 9am–5pm'? The correct and simple way to express ranges of time or distance or temperature is of course '*from ... to*' and it is hard to find a reason for its not being used in these examples other than plain stupidity.

between you and I *Between*, *from* and *to* are prepositions and take the accusative form of the noun. Even the many people who are unaware of this basic grammatical rule would not dream of saying 'The distance *between we and* that hill' or '*From I to you*' or '*To I and* my wife'. Yet all too often nowadays we find people saying, or even writing, '*Between you and I*' or '*From the wife and I*' or '*To Maggie and I*'. This oddity, which is sometimes

21

referred to as 'the toff's error', was noted as long ago as the 1930s but seems to have become much more common in the last twenty or so years. Presumably it arises from a feeling of discomfort about using the word *me*, a sense that it is somehow impolite or 'uneducated'. It may be that this has arisen from hearing other people saying '*Me* and Bill went down the pub'. Whatever the reason, it is because this is such a major misapprehension, and such an egregious example of Bad English being used under the impression that it is somehow better than the English one would naturally speak and write, that we have used it as the title of this book.

See also ME, US, HIM/HER, THEM.

bored of   We are *bored by* or *bored with* something or somebody. It is not at all good English to be *bored of* something or somebody (probably by analogy with 'tired of'), although this usage has become increasingly common, especially among the young.

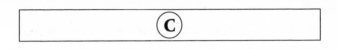

careen   In American fiction in particular we often find such a statement as 'The car *careened* down the street'. Users of this expression may be surprised to discover that the original meaning of *to careen* is to turn a vessel over on its side so that its bottom may be scraped clean of barnacles etc., or for a vessel, in turning sharply, to expose one side of its hull almost completely. What they presumably mean to convey is the idea of something rushing headlong down a street on a dangerously erratic course. Using *careen* in this false sense may well have resulted from the conflation of two other words: *career*, which means 'to rush headlong', and the old word *carom*, which is what a billiard ball does when it collides with another ball.

In American English, *careen* is certainly a Lost Cause, since its use in this erroneous sense is recognised in dictionaries, but for British English it may not be too late to rescue it.

centre   'The tragedy of Oedipus *centres around* the fact that he has unknowingly killed his father and married his mother.' Things have their *centre* at a particular point and not *around* it; therefore Oedipus's tragedy should *centre on* his unfortunate relationship with his parents.

change, sea, step   Nowadays, it seems, it is impossible for a politician or a public spokesman of any kind to refer to a simple 'change' or even to a 'major change'; it must be a *sea change* or a *step change*.

A *sea change* is the kind of mysterious change wrought by long immersion in the sea which results in something quite unrecognisable, the reference of course being to Shakespeare's *The Tempest*: 'But doth suffer a *sea change*, into something rich and strange.'

A *step change* is a technical expression, referring to a change to an entirely different order, for example of number, such as from tens to thousands.

Most of the *changes* announced or promised by politicians are neither of the *sea* nor of the *step* variety.

24

chauvinism   The word is derived from Nicolas Chauvin, a Napoleonic veteran noted, and in the end derided, for his extreme, unquestioning patriotism. The notion has long been extended into an unshakeable conviction of the superiority of any group or cause at the expense of other groups or causes; hence *economic chauvinism*, *white chauvinism* and (since 1970) *male chauvinism*.

Most users of the last of these terms, perhaps coming on the word for the first time and ignorant of its earlier meaning, drop the *male* and refer simply to *chauvinism*. However, since there is still plenty of *chauvinism* of the old sort around, it might seem worth while to try to preserve the word in its original sense, adding *white* or *male* as appropriate.

cohort   A *cohort* was a unit of the Roman Army roughly equivalent to a battalion in modern armies. Later the word came to denote a number of persons united in a common cause or for a common purpose, or simply 'supporters', 'attendants' or whatever. For some time it has had a technical use in demographics as a group of persons having a statistical characteristic in common, particularly that of being born in the same year.

What it does not mean is 'an associate' or 'an accomplice', as in the sentence, 'X was found guilty, along with his three *cohorts*'. If the word is correctly used, a *cohort* cannot be a single person.

collateral damage   A piece of euphemistic jargon which attempts to obscure through the use of 'cool', abstract language the reality of death, maiming and destruction of property among the civilian population as an unintended consequence of military action. For other euphemisms of this kind, see also for example FRIENDLY FIRE.

commence   Except in formal contexts it is better to avoid this word and instead to use one of its humbler synonyms, *start* and *begin*.

community   Rarely has a fine, even a noble, word been so devalued in recent times as this one has.

A *community* is a group of people living in close proximity and sharing their resources, to the extent even of eating at a common table. There were, and are, religious *communities* and 'alternative' *communities* which live in this way. In a slightly looser sense there are village or neighbourhood *communities* in which people know each other by name, go to each other's weddings and funerals, and share in communal activities such as village fetes and street parties; the radio serial *The Archers* and the television serials *Coronation Street* and *East-Enders* might be said to represent such *communities* in fictional form. Until quite recent times it was just about legitimate to write about 'the Hollywood *community*', in that the stars, the producers and the directors lived in close proximity, knew one another, met in the same restaurants and clubs, and were in a position to exchange fresh rather than warmed-up or recycled gossip.

But now we have the 'gay *community*', the 'Asian *community*', the 'financial *community*' and even the 'Arts *community*'; phrases referring to large numbers of people widely dispersed geographically, mostly unknown to one another, and united only by such factors as sexual orientation, ethnicity, skill at making money out of money, or an interest

27

in seeking subsidies from the taxpayer for cultural activities which would otherwise be unsustainable; in short, not *communities* in any real sense at all.

There are of course Asian, gay and artistic *communities* in the true sense of the word, but that is a quite different matter. For general purposes it should be enough to say 'most Asians', 'most gays' etc.

compare to/with   Since the *com* part of *compare* means 'with' it might be thought that it was always correct to say *'compare with'* and wrong to say *'compare to'*. Those who believe this would have to answer to, among others, William Shakespeare, who wrote 'Shall I *compare* thee *to* a summer's day?' The rule of thumb is that *compare to* is correct when you are drawing attention to the similarities between two objects ('Shall I *say that you resemble* a summer's day?'). *Compare with* is to be preferred when we wish to note differences as well as or rather than similarities, as in *'Compared with* its mighty and quarrelsome neighbours, Ruritania is a quaint, untroubled, rather backward little country.'

Shakespeare, of course, goes on to say that no, he won't *compare* his mistress *to* a summer's day, and explains why not by conducting a detailed *comparison with* summer, in which the lady emerges as better in every respect – 'more lovely and more temperate'.

comprise, compose   These two words bear a close relationship without being identical when correctly used. The basic rule is that the parts *compose* the whole; the whole *comprises* (or *consists of* or *is composed of*) the parts. Thus 'A full pack *comprises* 52 cards', but 'A good society is a means to a good life for those who *compose* it'. (Bertrand Russell, quoted in the *Shorter Oxford English Dictionary*.)

This distinction has been weakening for half a century or more, perhaps without much harm being done. But the typical estate agent's phrase 'The property comprises *of* two reception rooms and four bedrooms with en suite' is seriously wrong and should be resisted; the same applies to the variant *'is comprised of'*. The correct alternatives would be *'comprises* two reception rooms' or *'consists of ...'* or *'is composed of ...'*.

29

consensus   This is how the word should be spelt. It derives from Latin words meaning something like 'the common feeling', hence 'general agreement'. The common spelling error *concensus* probably stems from confusion with *census* ('the official count of a population'), which has a quite different derivation.

contemporary   Since at least the 17th century, *contemporary* has meant living or occurring at the same time, but there is a built-in ambiguity here: it can mean 'living at the same time as each other', as in 'Shakespeare was a contemporary of the composer John Dowland', or it can mean 'living or occurring at the same time as us who are living now'.

A difficulty arises from the fact that *contemporary* entered the popular lexicon at about the same time as the Festival of Britain (1951) with reference to the design style of that era, which mainly had to do with striped wallpaper, coffee tables with splayed legs and the practice of using different wallpaper patterns on different walls in the same room. *Contemporary* as a result became associated with the 'modernity' of that era and for a while could scarcely be used without further qualification.

Because of its built-in ambiguity the word must be used with care. If a production of Shakespeare's *The Tempest* with *contemporary* music is announced, does this mean music by his *contemporary* John Dowland or by our *contemporary* composer Sir Harrison Birtwistle? (We should be warned.)

coruscate   In the print and broadcasting media, a review of a book or a play is frequently described as *coruscating*. The user of this word presumably does not mean to suggest that the review is flattering, and is therefore on the face of it unaware that *to coruscate* means 'to glitter, to throw off flashes of light'.

Some of the theatre reviews of the late Kenneth Tynan might correctly have been described as *coruscating*, but if the writer means to suggest that a review is designed to cause severe pain, the word he or she is almost certainly looking for is *excoriating*, from 'to *excoriate*', meaning 'to flay, or to strip or rub the flesh off'.

31

could of   Educated readers will not need to be told that *could of* represents an illiterate mishearing of *could have* and can never, in any circumstances, be correct English.

crescendo   This is a musical term meaning a steady increase in volume of sound. (*Crescendo* is an Italian word meaning simply 'increasing'.) Since by definition a *crescendo* is a process which ends with maximum volume, it makes no sense to say that 'the music was approaching its *crescendo*' or that 'the violence reached a *crescendo*' as if the word meant 'a peak' or 'a climax'.

criterion   *Criterion* is a singular noun of Greek origin. Its plural is *criteria*. There are a great many supposedly educated people, including for example the 'Education Correspondent' of the *Daily Telegraph* (21 November 2001), who seem to be unaware of this elementary fact.

See also PHENOMENON.

daily basis, on a   See BASIS, ON A ...

dangling participle   'Walking up the familiar drive, the house seemed strangely quiet.'

This is an example of a dangling, or unattached, participle. It offends against common sense as well as against the rules of grammar (which should after all have a basis in common sense), since obviously it is not the house that is walking up the drive but the person who is telling the tale. Writing 'Walking up the familiar drive, I noticed that ...' would have re-attached the participle to its proper subject, 'I', and saved the sentence from being nonsensical.

Here is another example, slightly more complicated but equally wrong, from a Home Office advertisement in *The Times* (quoted in Burchfield, *The New Fowler's Modern English Usage*): 'By giving this youngster the chance to repair and race old cars, he's not tempted to steal new ones.' This might with advantage have read: 'Our hope is that, by giving this youngster the chance to repair and race old cars, we'll help him to resist the temptation to steal new ones.' In this latter version, the participial phrase 'by giving this youngster the chance ...' has been re-attached to what it qualifies: '... we'll help him to resist ...'.

Examples of dangling or unattached participles abound in today's newspapers and broadcast media and even in books from respected publishers. Once recognised, they should be instantly zapped by the laser beam of common sense.

data   The word *data* is a Latin plural of which the singular, *datum*, is nowadays very rarely used. In its modern meaning of 'results in the form of facts and figures' it should, strictly speaking, be used with a plural verb, but in the world of computing it has become a singular noun, taking a singular verb.

decimate   The word is obviously related to *decimal*, both being based on the Latin word for the number ten. The ancient Romans dealt with mutiny or cowardice in the army by selecting one man in ten, chosen by lot, for punishment, which normally meant death. *Decimated* is now often used instead of some such word as *devastated*, but should not be. When environmental activists claim that seals or other sea creatures are at risk of being *decimated* by an oil spill from a tanker, they presumably mean to suggest that many more than one in ten are likely to be killed or disabled. Statements such as 'This small Palestinian township has been *decimated* in the recent conflicts' are equally unhelpful and misleading.

To *devastate*, by the way, means 'to ruin utterly, to turn into a wasteland'. In an age when such claims are often made it might be useful to have a word that means something more than *decimated* but less than *devastated*.

defuse, diffuse   To *defuse* is literally to remove the fuse from an explosive device and figuratively to remove the tension from a potentially dangerous situation. To *diffuse* is to disperse. The two words should not be confused but frequently are, particularly in the 'quality' newspapers.

déjà vu   The French phrase, meaning literally 'already seen', is correctly used to denote the feeling most of us have from time to time that we have seen or experienced something before, although in fact we are seeing or experiencing it for the first time. It is quite often wrongly used, especially by broadsheet journalists, to refer to something that has become boring or old hat because it has been seen or experienced once too often. If one wishes to use a French phrase for this, the correct one is *vieux jeu*.

deprecate, depreciate   These two words have quite distinct meanings but are frequently confused.

To *deprecate* (from a Latin word meaning, literally, 'to pray away' and hence 'to ward off through prayer') is 'to deplore, to heartily wish that something were elsewhere or otherwise than it is'. In our time it has become familiar in a milder form as *self-deprecating*, which we can perhaps understand by imagining someone modestly waving away attention from him- or herself: 'I pray you, pay no attention to little old *moi*!'

To *depreciate* likewise comes from a Latin word, in this case meaning 'to lower the price'. We can *depreciate* someone, in the sense of lowering or underestimating his or her worth, and our cars can, and mostly do, *depreciate* in the sense that they decrease in value.

derisive, derisory   The two words are complementary, not synonymous in correct modern usage. *Derisive* means 'mocking'; *derisory* means 'causing *derision*, ridiculous', as in 'Management's latest offer is *derisory*. My members will greet it with *derisive* laughter.'

deteriorate   This is a Latinate word meaning simply 'to get worse'. If it is to be used at all it should be pronounced with all five syllables and not as *deteriate*.

diagnose   'She was *diagnosed* with cancer.'

This is an odd one. We dig with a spade, we eat with cutlery, we play golf with golf clubs. Yet for some reason we *diagnose* with a disease, rather than with *diagnostic* skills or instruments, as might have been expected. Perhaps the usage derives from such expressions as 'He was down *with* 'flu' or 'She was crippled *with* arthritis'. Whatever the reason, this appears to be a Lost Cause, since the expression is nowadays used by medical 'experts' as well as by ignorant laymen, but readers might still prefer to say, '*diagnosed* as having …'.

didn't used   In John Lanchester's much admired novel *The Debt to Pleasure* (1996) it is surprising to find his pedantic and supposedly erudite hero using the phrase 'It *didn't used* to be' (along with a number of other historical and linguistic howlers, but no doubt the book is 'post-modern' and 'ironic'). This expression is extremely common, but if it were correct it would be the only occasion on which *didn't* is not followed by the infinitive form of the verb. We say '*didn't* walk', '*didn't* buy', '*didn't* go'; we don't say '*didn't* walked, '*didn't* bought', '*didn't* went'. So why do we say '*didn't* used'?

It may be that the answer is that the verb 'to use' in the sense of 'to do as a customary practice' is never encountered in the present tense. We are 'used to' saying that someone 'used to' be or do something. Therefore when we hear someone, correctly, say something like 'He *didn't use* to wear gloves' (as Peter Cheney wrote in 1964) we have grown accustomed to hearing it as '*didn't used ...*'. It is, nevertheless, an illiterate form of words that educated people should avoid, at least in writing.

different than That glorious book and national treasure, R.W. Burchfield's *The New Fowler's Modern English Usage* (Oxford University Press, Revised Third Edition 1998) is surprisingly tolerant of *different than* (and of *different to*). While recognising that *different than* is commoner in American than in British English, in gently challenging those who would claim that it can never be 'Good English', Burchfield uses powerful ammunition in the form of citations in the *Oxford English Dictionary* from as early as 1644, and he dismisses in his typically elegant yet kindly manner the argument that we say 'x *differs from* y' and not 'x *differs than* y' or 'x *differs to* y', giving examples of other inconsistencies of that kind which are regarded as perfectly acceptable.

It is true that *than* normally follows a comparative, as in 'bigger *than*', 'faster *than*' etc. *Different* is not a comparative; its comparative form is 'more *different*'. No pedant could possibly quarrel with the sentence, 'No two brothers could be more *different* in temperament *than* Cain and Abel', just as no pedant could accept the sentence, 'Cain was *different than* Abel'.

However, *than* also follows such non-comparatives as *rather* and *other*, and it is here that counsel for the defence of *different than* might find a chink through which a case for legitimacy might be made. It may well be that if *different than*, however mistaken, survives and prospers, it is because from time to time it avoids awkwardness of construction. Burchfield quotes a good example of this from *The Oxford Guide to English Usage* (1993): 'Compare *The American Theatre, which is suffering from a different malaise than ours*, which is greatly preferable to *suffering from a different malaise from that which ours is suffering from.*'

Nevertheless, Burchfield's conclusion is that 'A wiser course, perhaps, is simply to avoid *different than* if you happen to be writing (or speaking) in

Britain'. We are happy, and grateful, to be able to agree with him.

dilemma   The expression 'the horns of a *dilemma*' refers figuratively to a situation in which if a man manages to avoid one of the horns of an angry bull he is bound to be impaled on the other. This vividly illustrates the correct meaning of the word *dilemma*, which was once a term in logic but now denotes a situation in which one has to make a choice between two options, both of which have severe disadvantages.

Although etymologically there should be only two options, some authorities are nowadays willing to allow three or more, provided that they are known and can be stated. The important point, however, is that *dilemma* does not mean simply 'a problem' or 'an awkward decision to have to make'.

discreet and discrete   *Discreet* means 'unobtrusive, circumspect, tactful'. *Discrete* means 'individually distinct, separate'. Some writers, and even some publishers' editors, seem to be under the

41

impression that *discrete* is a more up-market way of spelling *discreet*. If so, they are mistaken.

Note that the noun from *discreet* is *discretion*; the noun from *discrete* is *discreteness*.

disincentivise   See INCENTIVISE.

disingenuous   See INGENIOUS, INGENUOUS.

disinterested   This is such an old favourite – in the 1980s it was the subject of more letters of complaint to the BBC than any other word, with the possible exception of *hopefully* – that one would expect everyone to know by now that *disinterested* ought to be used only in the sense of 'impartial, having nothing personally to gain or lose', especially as the sense of 'finding uninteresting, being bored by' is perfectly well served by *uninterested*. Nonetheless what many old-fashioned people regard as a grave crime is still committed daily in speech and in print.

According to R.W. Burchfield in *The New Fowler's*, the matter is not quite as cut and dried as it appears, but it is surely a matter of practical common sense to preserve two separate words for two distinct meanings.

discuss We *discuss* something; we do not *discuss about* something.

disparate *Disparate* can mean either 'markedly, essentially different' or – its older but nowadays rather less common sense – 'unequal', as in 'countries of *disparate* size'. What it does not mean is merely *different*.

dissect To *dissect* is 'to cut apart'. The *dis-* is the same as the *dis-* in *dismember* and *dislocate* and many other words, and that is how the word should be pronounced. To pronounce it as *die-sect* is ignorant. The word *bisect* (to cut in two) is not a helpful analogy.

downsizing Euphemistic jargon for scaling down a commercial enterprise, almost invariably by means of cutting the numbers of staff employed in it.

See also LET GO, TO.

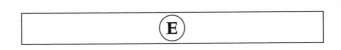

either ... or   If only for the sake of clarity *either* and *or* should be placed as closely as possible before the alternatives they refer to. For example, 'He was determined to acquire *either* wealth *or* fame, and preferably both' is much better English than 'He was *either* determined to acquire wealth *or* fame, and preferably both'.

The same principle applies to *neither ... nor*.

enervate   To *enervate* is to deprive of nerve in the sense of spirit, energy or courage; to be *enervated* is to be weakened or spiritless. Writers and speakers sometimes use the word *enervated* as if it were a synonym for *invigorated* or *energised*, but they could hardly be more mistaken.

envy and jealousy   We are *jealous* of what is our own. We *envy* what belongs to others. Othello was driven to murder by strong sexual *jealousy* concerning his wife; in poisoning his mind against her, Iago was perhaps motivated by *envy* of Othello's glorious reputation as a successful general.

epicentre   *Epicentre* comes from Greek words meaning 'upon a point' and is a technical term for the point on the earth's surface immediately above the point of origin of an earthquake. To use it as if it were an up-market substitute for the ordinary word *centre* – as in 'Basingstoke is the *epicentre* of Arts activity in the region' – is to invite ridicule.

equally as   It is correct to say 'The two men are *equally* stupid' or 'One is *as* stupid *as* the other'. It is quite wrong to conflate *equally* and *as* into 'One is *equally as* stupid as the other'.

equate   We *equate* one thing *with* another; we do not *equate* one thing *to* another.

exclusive   Things are *exclusive* by virtue of the fact that they *exclude*. An *exclusive* club excludes people not deemed suitable for election to membership. An *exclusive* hotel or resort excludes people who cannot afford its prices.

In the commercial world the word *exclusive* has come to mean ... either virtually nothing, as in Marks and Spencer's advertising slogan '*Exclusively* for everyone', or some such notion as that 'It looks much more expensive than it actually is'.

If I receive in the post an '*exclusive* offer' why is it that so many of my neighbours have also received it?

executive   An *executive* is someone who carries things out or gives effect to policy, nowadays often specifically a member of a relatively senior tier of management. So what is '*executive* housing', and what is an '*executive* car' or an '*executive* lounge'? Used in this way, *executive* seems to be a codeword meaning 'indicative of a certain level of salary and of a "lifestyle" that is reassuringly middle class'.

expatriate   As a noun the word denotes someone living outside his or her own country and is so spelt and not as *ex-patriot*, which, if it existed as a word, would presumably mean 'a former patriot'.

fascination   Broadly speaking this means either 'the action or faculty of compelling attention' or 'the state of being *fascinated*'. Snakes, supposedly, can *fascinate* their victims into a state of passivity by holding them with their eyes. However, care needs to be taken with this word. If we have a *fascination with* goldfish we quickly become absorbed in watching them and find it difficult to tear ourselves away. But if we have a *fascination for* goldfish they are irresistibly drawn to watching *us*. We should be clear about which of these two things we mean.

February   This word has four syllables, the second of which begins with an *r*, but one would scarcely know this from the way it is pronounced by many speakers of British English.

fine-toothed comb   This is often sounded as if it were '*a fine toothcomb*' as in 'They went through the documents with a *fine toothcomb*'. So what

49

exactly is a *toothcomb*? What is meant, of course, is a *fine-tooth* or *fine-toothed comb*, one capable, metaphorically, of thorough sifting or searching.

flout and flaunt 'Saddam Hussein has continued to *flaunt* UN resolutions.' (Tom Carver, BBC Washington Correspondent, September 2002)

At the time of writing the only UN resolutions that Saddam Hussein would be likely to *flaunt* would be those that forbade any interference in his country's internal affairs. The BBC correspondent almost certainly meant to say *flout*.

To *flaunt* is 'to display ostentatiously'. To *flout* is 'to break (rules or regulations) openly and even with contempt'. The two words are very often confused, but should not be.

forensic This rather technical word means something like 'pertaining to courts of law, legal argument, the procurement of evidence for a court of law etc.' *Forensic* medicine is medicine in the service of the court, but the word *forensic* by itself has nothing to do with medicine or with medical investigation.

fortuitous   The word means 'produced by chance, accidental', from the Latin word *forte*, 'by chance'. *Fortuitous* does not mean 'fortunate' and *fortuitously* does not mean 'by happy chance', but an increasing number of speakers and writers seem to be unaware of this.

fraught   People who describe a situation as *fraught* seem to know what they mean to say, and people who hear them seem to understand what they are saying: that the situation is 'distressing' perhaps, or 'stressful', or just 'tricky'. They would probably be surprised to know that the original meaning of the word is 'freighted' or 'laden', so that a situation could at least in theory be *fraught* with delightful possibilities as well as with difficulties.

It is better to avoid the word unless we can say what something is *fraught* with, and it is never right to refer to 'a *fraught* situation'.

free gift   Next time you are offered a *free gift*, ask yourself – or better still, the party offering it – whether there is any other kind, a *gift* being something that is given, not sold.

free rein   To give *free rein* is to allow someone a considerable amount of freedom of action. The term comes from horse-riding and should be spelt *free rein* and not *free reign*, although the latter phrase, presumably meaning 'unhindered rule', may have possibilities.

friendly fire   Euphemism for fire originating from one's own side during military conflict as a result of misidentification, panic or incompetence. The term was current during the war in Vietnam but became more widely known during the Gulf War of 1991 when, as in the Iraq conflict of 2003, several deaths and injuries were attributed to it. The expression strikes many as tasteless, but to date no one has come up with a more dignified alternative that has the same neatness.

See also COLLATERAL DAMAGE.

fulsome   Since the 17th century the word has meant 'excessively flattering, unctuous', as in the manner of Charles Dickens's Pecksniff towards those with whom he wishes to ingratiate himself. In the last half century, however, it has been increasingly used, mainly by politicians and journalists, as if it meant simply 'full, generous', as in 'a *fulsome* apology' or 'a *fulsome* tribute'. Burchfield also notes its use by fashion writers to mean 'full-figured', perhaps by analogy with *handsome* or *wholesome*. The older meaning should be preserved, if only because it cannot so easily be replaced.

gerund, the   This is certainly a Lost Cause, at least in the sense that very few people nowadays know what a *gerund* is. But just as people still use the *subjunctive* form (especially in American English) without knowing the term itself – 'He insisted that she *go* to bed immediately' – so the *gerund* survives in use, although largely unrecognised. The *gerund* is derived from a verb, usually by adding the suffix *-ing.* Although remaining a verb, it acts in some respects as if it were a noun, and especially in the respect that if the action denoted is attributed to someone or something it needs to be accompanied by the possessive form. A few examples should make this clearer: it is correct to say 'We were surprised at *their* appearing so calm', 'She was distressed at *his* leaving so suddenly', 'I was surprised at *its* being so easy to do'. It would be wrong to say '*them* appearing', '*him* leaving', '*it* being'.

graffiti   Not many people in Britain, it seems, know that the word *graffiti* is the plural of the Italian *graffito*, meaning, originally, 'a scratched inscription or drawing'. *Graffiti* should therefore be used with a plural verb, but rarely is, even by supposedly educated speakers and writers.

Conversely, a single spray-painted slogan should be termed a *graffito*.

ground rules   Correctly, the special *rules* pertaining to a particular playing-*ground*, course or court – because, for example, of special physical features or size restrictions – and not, as widely supposed, the basic or fundamental *rules*.

guttural   This should be so spelt, and not as *gutteral*. It is a term in phonetics denoting a sound produced in the throat and should not be used as if it meant simply 'harsh, not mellifluous'.

harass, harassment   Educated speakers of British English place the stress on the first syllable. Others do not.

hare-brained   This should be so spelt, the reference being to the apparently crazy behaviour of *hares* in the mating season. To spell it as *hair-brained* is an error.

hierarchy   Note that this, and not *heirarchy*, is the correct spelling. It may help to know that the *hier-* part of the word derives from a Greek word meaning 'sacred' or 'priestly'. The fact that *hier-* sounds like 'higher' is no doubt partly responsible for its having long ago strayed from its older meaning so as to include the notion of 'ranking, order', as in 'the corporate *hierarchy*'.

hoi polloi   These Greek words mean 'the many, the common people, the vulgar masses', *hoi* being the masculine plural of the definite article *the*. In English, it is an excusable mistake to say or write 'the *hoi polloi*'. However, it is not excusable to suppose, as some writers seem to do, that *hoi polloi* means 'the rich, the plutocracy, the upper social set'.

homogeneous   The word, meaning 'of the same kind', should be so spelt, with five syllables, and pronounced with the stress on the third syllable. It should not be confused, in spelling or pronunciation, with the scientific word *homogenous* (in biology or comparative anatomy, 'having a common descent'), but often is.

homophobia   This word seems to have been coined at some time during the 1970s to mean 'fear or hatred of homosexuals, or of homosexuality'. The persons responsible for coining it and putting it into circulation may or may not have been aware that the *homo-* part of the word *homosexual* derives from the Greek word *homos* meaning 'the same', so that, strictly speaking, *homophobia* ought to mean 'fear or hatred of things that are the same', perhaps

58

the philosophy of those who believe that 'variety is the spice of life'.

However repugnant to lovers of the classical languages, *homophobia* must now be accounted a Lost Cause, if only because no one has been able to come up with an alternative, inoffensive word for a sentiment or attitude that seems to have been unknown to the ancient Athenians.

homosexual   A government minister recently announced that the word *homosexual* was to be banned from all government communications because it was 'offensive'. It is hard to see why, or to think of a more neutral, 'value-free' way of denoting the condition of being 'sexually drawn to one's own sex'. It may be that there are still people who believe that the *homo-* part of the word comes from the Latin *homo* (which in any case means 'human being' rather than 'male'), whereas in fact it comes from the Greek *homos,* meaning 'the same'.

One can indicate an awareness of this by pronouncing the first syllable to rhyme with 'Tom' rather than with 'home'.

hopefully   Since the 1960s *hopefully* has been the favourite bugbear of language purists when used in such sentences as '*Hopefully* it will be over by Christmas'. It is strange that this particular adverb should be singled out for hatred and ridicule in the way that it has, for its case is by no means unique.

Consider the following sentences: '*Frankly* I could do without it'; '*Sadly*, he died before I managed to reach him again'; '*Fortunately* I had enough money left to pay my fare home'. It should be evident that these three adverbs do not directly qualify the verb in the sentence in which they appear. Instead they qualify the whole of the statement to which they are attached, indicating the spirit in which it is made. They are in fact sentence adverbs, and they could be said to be shorthand for longer expressions such as 'To speak *frankly*' or 'I am *sad* to say that ...' or 'It was *fortunate* that ...'. Robert Burchfield in *The New Fowler's Modern English Usage* explains that they have been used in this way since the 17th century but that the usage has become much more common since the 1960s. It may be that *hopefully*'s crime has been to be a relatively recent newcomer to the ranks of the sentence adverbs and to have come to us from the United States, but it is not at all clear that it deserves the condemnation it so often receives.

hyphen　　When verb phrases are used as nouns, it is usual and correct to insert a hyphen, as in for example *start-up*, *lay-offs*, *set-up*, *take-off*, *take-over*. It is sad to see how few editors realise that when these nouns revert to being verb phrases the hyphen is no longer needed and should go. It is ignorant to write 'They intend to *start-up* a new company', 'They are expected to *lay-off* some of the older workers' etc.

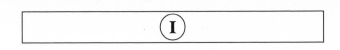

ilk   This good Scots word means 'same', as in the name Glenporridge *of that Ilk*, i.e. Glenporridge of that same, or in other words Glenporridge, (Laird) of Glenporridge. It does not mean 'like' or 'sort'. So when people talk or write of 'persons of that ilk' rather than 'persons like that' in the belief that they are using a rather superior form of speech they are in fact displaying ignorance.

immanent, imminent   The two words look and sound alike, but should not be confused.

Immanent means 'inherent, pervading (creation or the universe)' and is most often found in religious or metaphysical contexts.

Imminent means simply 'about to happen'.

imply, infer   In explaining the important difference between these two words it is probably impossible to improve on the example given by A.P. Herbert in *What a Word* (1935): 'If you see a man staggering along the road you may *infer* that he is drunk, without saying a word, but if you say "Had one too many?" you do not *infer* but *imply* that he is drunk.'

In case any doubt remains, here is another example: 'I *infer* from what you say that you do not believe my statement; you seem to *imply* that my word is not to be trusted.'

In other words, *infer* means 'deduce', and should not be used to mean *imply*, though it very often is.

incentivise   Anyone with an ear for language will want to avoid this hideous recent coinage, meaning, presumably, 'to give an incentive to', and its counterpart, *disincentivise*, meaning, presumably, 'to withhold or withdraw an incentive'. Both were used by 'a government advisor on pension matters and governor of the London School of Economics' on the BBC's 'Today' programme on 21 October 2002.

in-depth   To refer to an '*in-depth* analysis' is not exactly Bad English, but never to use the word 'analysis' without attaching *in-depth* to it is another example of auto-pilot English. The 'analysis' could also be *thorough* or *exhaustive*, or for that matter *sloppy* or *superficial*.

industry   Not long ago, one sense of the word *industry* was in reference to the activity of manufacturing concerns, whether *heavy*, as in coal-mining, steel-making, ship-building etc., or *light*, as in pharmaceuticals, textiles etc.; in short, the kind of manufacturing activity that involved numbers of 'manual' workers.

At some time in the 1960s, many people of the kind Marxists used to call 'workers by brain' seem to have decided to claim their share of the nobility of labour by designating their activities as '*industrial*'. Thus we now have 'the financial services *industry*', 'the publishing *industry*', 'the classical music *industry*', 'the Bloomsbury *industry*', 'the Sylvia Plath *industry*' and so forth. As the United Kingdom's manufacturing base shrinks further and further, readers might be justified in suspecting that there is some kind of compensation mechanism at work here.

ingenious, ingenuous   These are two very similar words with quite distinct meanings that should not be confused.

The current meaning of *ingenious* is 'clever or skilful in a sense suggestive of complexity or intricacy', as in 'an *ingenious* device' or 'a most *ingenious* criminal'.

Ingenuous means 'frank, open, artless, even naive'.

To be *disingenuous* is in effect to be a great deal less *ingenuous* than one is pretending to be.

The noun from *ingenious* is, oddly enough, *ingenuity*; the noun from *ingenuous* is *ingenuousness*.

in terms of   Properly used, this prepositional phrase declares the terms in which a statement is claimed to be true: '*In terms of* numbers of men, tanks and other *matériel*, the French in the spring of 1940 were superior to the German forces opposing them; *in terms of* other factors, such as *morale* and communications, they were, as it soon turned out, sadly inferior.'

In terms of is still occasionally used correctly in this way, but in recent times it has started to behave like an irresistible virus, destroying and replacing such old familiar words and phrases as *concerning* or *as regards* or *in view of* or *in the light of* or even simply *about*, to the extent that one now seems to hear or read it a hundred times a day.

One very recent example demands to be quoted: discussing a cricketer's decision not after all to play for the English touring team, a speaker on BBC radio declared that 'his attitude is not surprising *in terms of* the personal crisis he has been going through'. Not long ago he would surely have said '*in view of* …'.

Perhaps this is not yet a Lost Cause. Perhaps *in terms of* is one of those modish phrases that sooner or later become wearisome through repetition. Perhaps before not too long it will be thought naff to ask 'What's your opinion *in terms of* Gordon Brown?' Let us hope so.

irregardless   This clownish word is so well disguised as a sensible one that it quite often slips by unnoticed, used in place of *regardless* – as in '*irregardless* of the consequences' – whereas what it means literally is '*not regardless*'. It is presumably a

conflation of *regardless* and *irrespective* and is sometimes used in jest, sometimes in ignorance.

In a similar vein, a spokesman for local government chief executives recently stated that the
Government was 'paying scant *disregard*' to some
problem or other.

is repeated   'The question *is*, *is* whether …';
'The point *is*, *is* that …'; 'The fact of the matter *is*, *is*
that …'; even 'The difficulty *is*, *was* that …'

This mysterious, and quite meaningless, repetition of the word *is* (or *was*) was first noted by an
American scholar in the United States in 1971 but
may now be heard on the BBC countless times in
the course of a normal day. It has even been
recorded on the lips of such notable politicians as
David Owen, Nigel Lawson and Gerald Kaufman
(representing all the major British political parties!). Examples of it have been printed above with
a comma after the first *is*, to indicate a brief pause,
but it is frequently heard without any pause at all
between the *is*es.

It is frequently heard, but it is rarely if ever seen
in print, perhaps because to see it written is at once

68

to recognise its absurdity. So the question is, why do people repeat the word *is* (or *was* for that matter)? Could it be that in putting strong emphasis on the initial phrase – *'the point is!'* – they hear it in their heads as 'the *important* point, the point that I am trying to stress' and in doing so fail to notice that first *is*? If so, this is an explanation, but it is not an excuse. This is English that is not only bad, but stupid, and it should be mocked and jeered at until it disappears out of sheer embarrassment.

issue Newly appointed Director-General of the BBC Mark Thompson stated on 22 May that some people 'had *issues* with' that organisation.

The recent history of this word has been fascinating. A century or so ago it meant, as an intransitive verb, 'to come forth', as in 'the words that *issued* from his lips'. As a noun it meant 'that which comes forth', as in 'the *issue* of his loins', or it meant 'the outcome, the result', as in 'the *issue* was in doubt'. In a legal context it meant 'the point in question' and, by extension, 'a matter that is in contention or which remains to be decided'. By the late 19th century it had come also to mean 'an item given out or supplied', as in 'Army *issue*'.

In the course of the Second World War language purists became greatly exercised when that last usage led to what was regarded as the hideous verb formation *to issue with*, as in 'the men were *issued with* clean underwear', which certainly represented a real departure in meaning from the intransitive to the transitive. Rightly or wrongly, that meaning of the verb *to issue* is now firmly established.

What has happened more recently is that, in some circles at least, what was at one time the legal usage of the noun *issue* – 'question, matter to be decided' – has virtually replaced all the others. As used by such interest groups as the feminists it has now more or less displaced the words *question* and *problem*, so that we have such statements as 'I don't have any *issues* with that' or 'BBC radio drama is mainly *issue*-based' or 'she has *issues* around gender differentiation'.

This is not, strictly speaking, Bad English, but it is becoming wearisome, and we must hope that it is a fashion that will one day pass.

key The word *key* has long been used figuratively to suggest 'that which unlocks a mystery or removes an obstruction' or – no doubt from the idea of a *keystone* – 'central, indispensable, pivotal'. Recently, however, its use as an adjective has gone to absurd lengths to give us such expressions as 'this is absolutely *key*', which thoughtful people will certainly want to avoid.

kind of *Kind* is a noun, its plural is *kinds*; therefore the normal rules about singular and plural ought to apply to it. Yet phrases such as 'those *kind of* people' are almost commoner nowadays than the correct and logical usage, which would of course be 'that *kind of* person'.

It is almost as if *kind of* has been silently hyphenated into a kind of adjective, but there is no good reason for it, and educated speakers should stick to the logical practice.

Kind of is also used colloquially as an adverb in

ways that suggest that the speaker is giving only an approximate sense of what he or she wants to say, as in for example 'I felt *kind of* sad' or 'I *kind of* thought you wouldn't come' or 'It was *kind of* beige'. This is now an acceptable part of informal speech but should of course be avoided in more formal contexts.

latter   'He had four sons, the *latter* of whom died in infancy.' *Latter* in this sentence should be *last*. *The latter* should be used only of the second item of a pair, corresponding to *the former*.

lead   The past tense of the verb *to lead* is *led*, not *lead*. There is nothing logical about this – the past tense of *read* is *read*, not *red* – but it is how it is.

leading question   In a British or American court an alert judge will be quick to restrain counsel from asking a *leading question* of a witness. A *leading question* is one which suggests to the witness the answer that counsel is looking for: 'Did you then see the accused pull out a revolver and shoot Constable Bucket?' would be an example. The permissible question would be: 'What did you see then?'

Among lay people the phrase is used as if it meant an important or an intrusive question or one that required the person questioned to say more than he or she cared to, but none of these is its correct meaning.

less and fewer   *Less* describes quantity; *fewer* describes number. For example: 'For a healthy diet we should eat *less* sugar, salt and animal fat and *fewer* sweets and chocolates', or 'in order to weigh *less* we should consume *fewer* calories'. It is Bad English to write for example 'There were *less* accidents on Britain's roads last year than in any year since 1958'.

The normal rule is that *fewer* is used with nouns which have plurals and *less* is used with nouns which have no plural in ordinary discourse, such as 'sand', 'chatter', 'food', 'trouble', 'praise', 'oil'.

When we are describing a number itself, *less* is correct. Thus: '*Fewer* than fifty people were injured' but 'The eventual death-toll was *less* than twenty'.

See also AMOUNT, NUMBER.

let go, to   This is one of several current euphemisms, mainly of US origin, for dismissing someone from employment. What is offensive about it is the genteel pretence that one is allowing an employee to leave rather than firing him or her.

The word *euphemism* derives from a Greek word meaning 'Use of an auspicious word for an inauspicious one'. To quote R.W. Burchfield: 'The use of euphemisms can be traced back to the Middle Ages, but the prevalence of such evasive and concealing (or fair-sounding) terminology has never been more marked than in the cruel social and political areas of life in the 20c' (*The New Fowler's Modern English Usage*).

See also for example COLLATERAL DAMAGE.

liaise, liaison   These are sometimes found spelt *liase* and *liason* but should not be. They are incorrectly used if they lose the sense of a link or connection between two things or two parties.

licence, license   In British English, the noun is spelt *licence*, the verb is spelt *license*. In American English both are spelt *license*.

lie and lay   In standard British English *to lay* is a transitive verb, that is, one that takes an object, as in

'To *lay* a brick'; to *lie* is an intransitive verb, that is, one that does not take an object, as in 'We *lie* down'. The past tense of *lay* is *laid* ('We *laid* a brick') and so is the passive voice ('The brick was *laid*'); the past tense of *lie* is *lay* ('We *lay* down') and the perfect tense is *have lain*; being an intransitive verb it cannot have a passive form.

Expressions such as 'He was just *laying* there, dead drunk' are recognised regional usages, but are not standard English.

light year   If this expression is to be used it is important to recognise that it is a unit of distance – the distance that light travels in one year, or around 6 million million miles – and not of time.

like and as   See AS AND LIKE.

literally   'The Iranians are *literally* glued to their television screens.' (Correspondent on the BBC World Service during the closing days of the war in Iraq, April 2003)

Literally means ... *literally*. It means that we mean, to the letter, exactly what we are saying, or

76

in other words that we are not speaking figuratively. If, therefore, we say, 'I was *literally* climbing the walls with anxiety' or 'He was *literally* drowning in debt' or 'They were *literally* glued to their television screens', then we are using the word in *literally* the opposite of its correct sense and committing a serious abuse of our language.

loathe and loath   The verb *to loathe*, meaning 'to detest', as in 'I *loathe* broccoli', is so spelt, with the *th* sound 'voiced', as in *breathe*. The adjective, meaning 'reluctant', as in 'I was *loath* to depart', is correctly spelt as either *loath* or *loth*, with the *th* sound 'unvoiced', as in *breath*.

lowest common denominator   'The BBC seems to be trying to appeal to the lowest common denominator of public taste.' That may well be true, but the fact is that in mathematics the lowest common denominator is a relatively high number – the lowest common denominator of 2, 3, 4 and 6 is 12 – whereas the highest common factor is a relatively low number – the highest common factor of 12 and 18 is 6. But since this is no longer widely understood, and since the speaker or writer is trying to convey the idea of lowness rather than highness, this must be accounted a Lost Cause.

majority   The word *majority* should be used of numbers or of countable nouns, that is, nouns that have plurals, for example 'the *majority* of Americans'. It should emphatically not be used of uncountable nouns, as in for example 'he inherited the *majority* of the estate'. In that last case one should say and write 'the *major* part' or 'the *greater* part' or, quite simply, '*most*'.

may and might   'Even so, without the Depression and the calamitous effect upon Germany from the end of that year, the Nazi Party *may* well have broken up and faded into oblivion.' (Ian Kershaw, *Hitler 1889–1936*, italics added)

'A mentally ill man *may* not have committed suicide had he been kept in hospital, rather than been discharged to be cared for in the community.' (*Guardian*, 1990, italics added)

A tour guide addressing a coach party near Slough, Bucks: 'And there is Eton College where

Prince Charles *may* have gone to school' (italics added).

In all of these examples *may* should be *might*. This is not simply a matter of grammatical pedantry but of clarity and common sense. What the tour guide appears to say is that it is possible that, unknown to the British public, the Prince of Wales attended the famous public school convenient for one of the family homes in Windsor rather than, as we had thought, his father's alma mater, Gordonstoun. What he presumably *means* to say is that there *was* a possibility at one time that Charles would go to Eton.

In precisely the same way, Professor Kershaw, if taken literally, appears to suggest that it is possible that the Nazi party disappeared in 1929 and the *Guardian* that it is possible that the unfortunate man did not after all commit suicide. In all three cases, any ambiguity would have been removed simply by the use of *might* rather than *may*. The general rule is that *may* represents a possibility that still exists, while *might* represents a possibility that existed at some time in the past but did not materialise at that time.

It should be a matter of grave concern that the word *might* as the past tense of *may* seems to be in danger of disappearing from both written and spoken English. The cost, in terms of simple clarity of meaning, is considerable, as the above examples illustrate. The problem is exacerbated when 'quality' newspapers and leading academics (and their publishers' editors) make this elementary error and thereby set such a poor example to those who don't feel completely confident in their use of the language.

Is this a case like that of *between you and I*? Does the writer fear for some reason that the use of the word *might* is somehow incorrect or impolite? If so, readers, take courage! *Might* is (quite often) right.

me, us, him/her, them   'Gloaters jab fingers at *we* who opposed the war, saying we have been proved wrong.' (Polly Toynbee, *Guardian*, 16 April 2003, italics added)

'They sent my brother and *I* to boarding school.' (Rory Bremner on 'Desert Island Discs', April 2003)

'The sexual tension *between he* and Norris as Di Jordan seems bizarrely disconcerting.' (From a television review in the *Daily Telegraph* listings supplement)

A strange disease is afflicting supposedly educated writers and speakers of English, and the last of the three quotations above (which might be the first recorded case of a new variant) suggests that it is becoming even more virulent. It takes the form of extreme nervousness amounting almost to terror concerning the use of *me*, *us*, *him/her* and *them*, the accusative forms of the personal pronouns *I*, *we*, *he/she* and *they*. Did Polly Toynbee (or, just possibly, her editor at the *Guardian*) feel that to say 'jab fingers at *us*' would be somehow uncouth? Did the excellent Rory Bremner think that it would be ill-mannered to talk of 'my brother and *me*'? Without further investigation it is impossible to say. As for the reviewer in the *Daily Telegraph* listings supplement, if a quick cure cannot be found it is to be hoped that he or she has been quarantined to prevent further spreading of the disease.

See also BETWEEN YOU AND I.

media   'Television is a spiv *media*.' (Michael Grade, Chairman of the BBC, 22 May 2004)

It should go without saying, but does not, that *media* is the plural of *medium*. The word is most usually found nowadays as shorthand for 'the *media* of communication', that is, the print and broadcast *media*, often personified so as to include the people who own and work in these *media*. *Media* is nonetheless a plural noun and should be used with a plural verb, as in 'the *media* have less influence on voters than their owners would like to believe'. Statements such as 'the media was present in large numbers' should be avoided.

militate and mitigate   These two words have quite distinct meanings that should not be, but often are, confused.

To *militate* (usually followed by 'against') is 'to have weight, force or effect', as in 'Brilliant though he was, the notorious irregularities of his private life *militated* against his reaching the higher offices of government'.

To *mitigate* is 'to make less severe, to moderate', as in the '*mitigating* circumstances' that might persuade a judge to reduce the sentence on a convicted felon.

minuscule   This word, which nowadays means simply 'very small', used to have a very particular meaning, referring to small manuscript letters as distinct from large letters or capitals (*majuscule*). The important point is that it should be spelt *minuscule* and not, as so often, *miniscule*.

mission statements   No public body these days, it seems, feels it has done its duty until it has produced what it will probably call a 'mission statement' in the form of a participial phrase: 'Providing jobs and services' (typical town council), 'Working to make London safer' (The Metropolitan Police) and so forth. Two noticed recently are: 'Making knowledge work' (The University of Bradford) and 'Connecting people with God' (St Mary's Church of England, Islington, London).

What is it about these phrases that is so irritating? In the case of St Mary's, Islington, per-haps it is the sheer *naffness* of reducing the *raison d'être* of the Church to a glib commercial slogan, no doubt in the name of 'accessibility', 'relevance' or 'youth appeal'. More generally it may be a sense of the essential dishonesty of 'statements' which, like the verbless sentences of Prime Minister Tony Blair, are not really statements at all but merely vague aspirations for which no one can properly be held to account.

It might be an amusing game to invent more truthful versions of some of these statements; in the case of the first two mentioned above perhaps 'Spending lots of your money on creating jobs for our political supporters' and 'Trying to make London safer by charging around its streets in fast cars'.

moment in time, at this   This is an example of what might be called 'speaking on auto-pilot'. The phrase *this moment* automatically triggers the follow-up, *in time*. But if a *moment* is not *'in time'* then what is it in? For Einstein and his successors it might be important to make a distinction, but for ordinary mortals it is surely enough to say *at this moment* or even, simply, *now*.

myriad   This was originally a Greek word meaning 'ten thousand'. It long ago came to mean 'a very large number, uncountable', as in 'a *myriad* butterflies' and must be accounted a Lost Cause.

neither ... nor   See EITHER ... OR.

no sooner ... when/barely ... than It is surprising how often one reads sentences such as '*No sooner* had I got into the house *when* the telephone rang' or '*Barely* had she entered the room *than* she was spotted by her ex-husband'.

Simple common sense rather than any notion of grammatical correctness would surely suggest that the comparative *sooner* should be followed by *than* and that the simple adverb *barely* (or *scarcely* or *hardly*) should not be.

not enough ands   'The scandal was headline news, seriously damaging the credibility of the President, the Republican Party and giving a considerable boost to the lagging Democrats.'

'Southern Scotland, North and East England will remain dry.' (Typical BBC weather forecast)

Many readers would sense that there was something wrong with these sentences without being able immediately to say what the something was; it is in fact the absence of an *and* between 'the President' and 'the Republican Party' in the first sentence and between 'Scotland' and 'North' in the second. Once that *and* is inserted and the comma removed, the meaning of the sentence is clarified (and the rhythm greatly improved).

What has happened in sentences of this kind is that the writer, or perhaps the writer's editor, has somewhat mindlessly applied an editorial 'rule' which states that in a list of more than two items or elements all *ands* should be removed except the final one. This is a rather crude rule which the best writers of English have felt free to ignore when it suits them – imagine Wordsworth writing:

'Roll'd round in Earth's diurnal course,
With rocks, stones and trees.'

But in any case the rule has been misapplied in the examples given above. In the first sentence there are in fact two verbs after 'headline news' –

'damaging' and 'giving' – and the first verb is followed by only two items – 'the President' and 'the Republican Party' – which therefore demand to be linked by *and* rather than by a comma. In the weather forecast, 'North' is not a noun but one of two adjectives qualifying 'England'.

As with so many examples of Bad English in this book, errors of this kind have begun to crop up regularly only in the last twenty or thirty years, reflecting once again the triumph of half-educated over both educated and uneducated speech.

not only ... but also   As in the case of EITHER ... OR, it is important to place *not only* where it logically belongs, which generally means not dropping it in too early. For example, 'He *not only* wrote history *but also* light fiction' is wrong; the sentence should read 'He wrote *not only* history *but also* light fiction'.

'He *not only* wrote history *but also* gave piano lessons' is also correct.

not so much   This is perfectly good English provided that it is followed by *as* and not by *but*. '*Not* *so much* a job *as* a way of life' is good English; *'Not so much* a job *but* a way of life' is not.

nouns as verbs   One of the less welcome imports from North America is the practice of using nouns as verbs. *To impact, to source* (or *out-source*), *to task, to fast-track* are examples now encountered every day, and there will no doubt be many more by the time this book is in print. They are part of a dreadful new and actually rather sinister bureau-speak which deserves a book to itself because the way it displaces thought and subverts meaning needs more discussion than there is room for here. George Orwell encountered an earlier version of it which he analysed in his classic essay 'Politics and the English Language', reproduced in an appendix to the present volume.

nuclear   This is the adjective from *nucleus* and should be pronounced *new-clee-ar* or possibly *noo-clee-ar* but not *noo-cue-lar*.

off of   To say and write *off of*, as in 'It fell *off of* a lorry', is not acceptable in standard English. 'It fell *off* a lorry' is correct English irrespective of the truth or falsehood of the statement.

on a daily basis   See BASIS, ON A ...

ongoing situation   Another example of auto-pilot-speak. If a *situation* is not *ongoing* has it not ceased to be a *situation* at all?

only   The rule that *only* should be placed only before the word it is intended to qualify is one that is often broken even by the best writers, but there are occasions when failure to place it carefully can cause confusion.

The extent to which its placing can alter meaning was delightfully illustrated by Marghanita Laski in the *Observer* in April 1963 (quoted by Burchfield in *The New Fowler's*). She describes how

91

at her preparatory school pupils were asked to place *only* in every possible position in the sentence, 'The peacocks are seen on the western hills': '*Only* the peacocks …'; 'The *only* peacocks …'; 'The peacocks are *only* …' etc.

oral, verbal   The two words should not be confused.

Oral means literally 'of or with the mouth', hence, of a statement, 'spoken'.

Verbal means 'in words'. A *verbal* statement, agreement or whatever may be spoken or written. A *non-verbal* communication is one that manages without words.

outplacement   This is another euphemism for the dismissal of one or more employees in a bid to save costs.

See also, for example, LET GO, TO.

panacea   This derives from a Greek word meaning 'all-healing' or 'cure-all'; hence 'a universal remedy', whether literally, in a strictly medical sense, or metaphorically in a wider sense. However the word is used, it is a howler to say or write 'a *panacea* for all ills' or 'a universal *panacea*', since the idea of universality is already implicit in the word itself. For the same reason, it is an error to attach the word to a particular ailment, as in 'a *panacea* for the common cold'.

paradigm shift   'The Job: To work with patients, professional groups and others to achieve a *paradigm shift* in patients' experiences of healthcare in England.' (Appointments advertisement in the *Guardian*'s Society pages, 7 April 2004. Italics added)

What exactly is a *paradigm shift*? The term has a technical meaning in the philosophy of science, but here it seems to mean nothing more than 'a complete change' (presumably for the better). See also CHANGE, SEA, STEP

peninsula(r)   The noun is *peninsula*. *Peninsular* is the adjective, but is depressingly often used as if it were the noun.

perspicacious, perspicuous   These two words should either be used with great care or else avoided in favour of rather simpler synonyms such as *perceptive* and *lucid*, not least because some of the greatest writers have sometimes confused them and their derivatives.

To over-simplify somewhat, *perspicacious* can be used only of a person and means 'clear-sighted, discerning, shrewd'. The noun derived from it may be *perspicacity* or *perspicaciousness*.

Perspicuous is normally applied only to things and means, literally, 'easy to see through'; hence 'clear, lucid, easily understood'. The corresponding noun is either *perspicuity* or *perspicuousness*.

phenomenon   This is a noun of Greek origin; its plural form is *phenomena*, but, as with CRITERION, this simple fact seems to be beyond the mental competence of many politicians and 'media people'.

practice, practise   In standard British English, the noun is spelt *practice*; the verb is spelt *practise*. Since the two forms sound exactly the same when spoken, it might reasonably be asked whether this matters very much. The conservative response might well be the 'finger in the dyke' argument: 'allow people to spell words any way they like, even in apparently unimportant cases, and a collapse into total chaos follows soon after'. Another argument might be that preserving a difference between the noun and the verb in their written forms might from time to time prevent ambiguity, for example in legal documents.

prefer ... than   'I *prefer* to get wet *than* carry an umbrella' is Bad English. Correct usages are 'I would *rather* get wet *than* carry an umbrella' or 'I *prefer* to get wet *rather than* carry an umbrella' or 'I *prefer* getting wet *to* carrying an umbrella'.

prestige   At one time this word answered to its

Latin derivation and conveyed the sense of 'illusion or delusion', with special reference to the deceptive tricks of a juggler or what would nowadays be called a 'magician' or a 'conjuror'. By the 19th century it had acquired its present meaning of 'reputation', either 'glamorous' or, more recently, 'both glamorous and of thoroughly solid value', as in 'a prestige address' or a 'prestige car'.

The same history applies to the adjective *prestigious*. The change in meaning is great, but is perhaps not greatly to be regretted, since we have no word for *prestige* ... except *prestige*.

prevaricate, procrastinate   The two words are quite distinct in meaning.

To *prevaricate* is to do what politicians are particularly skilled at: avoiding a direct answer to a question, quibbling, acting evasively.

To *procrastinate* is to delay, to put off endlessly, *cras* being the Latin word for tomorrow.

principle, principal   These two words should not be confused, but often are.

Principle is only ever used as a noun, meaning 'a

fundamental truth or law as the basis of reasoning or action' as in 'He always stuck by his *principles*'.

Principal is either an adjective meaning 'most important, chief' or a noun referring to the chief person, for example the head teacher of an American school, or a leading character in a film or a play or, in a special sense, a capital sum as distinct from the interest earned from it.

prior to   This means nothing more or less than *before* and it is hard to think of circumstances in which it would not be better to say and write *before* rather than *prior to*.

privilege   Not long ago the National Association of Teachers of English urged an Education minister not to *privilege* standard English over regional and working-class dialects, meaning presumably that standard English should not be granted greater importance than non-standard English. Apart from the questionable wisdom of this advice, which would in effect limit the command of a universally comprehensible version of the language to a *privileged* minority, it is depressing to see *privilege* used as a verb in this way. Fortunately, however, the usage seems to be confined to the more fashionable and foolish elements of the academic 'community'.

See also NOUNS AS VERBS.

procrastinate   See PREVARICATE.

prophecy, prophesy   The noun is spelt *prophecy*; the verb is spelt *prophesy*.

protagonist   In Ancient Greek drama the *protagonist* was the principal actor. The *pro-* part of the word is from the Greek word *protos*, 'first', and there was originally only one *protagonist*.

Over the centuries it has become acceptable to use *protagonists* in the plural to mean the chief persons in a drama or in a situation. It is still wrong, however, to put the word *leading* or *main* or *chief* in front of it, since that is implicit in the first syllable, *pro-*.

What is even more wrong is to use the word to mean 'a supporter, a proponent, an advocate', as in 'She was an early *protagonist* of women's rights', on the mistaken assumption that the *pro-* is the Latin prefix meaning 'for, in favour of', and that therefore *protagonist* is the opposite of *antagonist*.

proven   Until relatively recently the word *proven* survived as a past participle in British English only in the Scottish legal verdict *not proven*. In the United States *proven* has long been at least as common as the usual British form of the past participle *proved*, and it is no doubt from there that it began to arrive here in the 1980s. Since then, like the American grey squirrel displacing the native red, *proven* has come almost to threaten the survival of the British form, especially in commercial contexts. Toothpastes are *proven* to leave teeth whiter, bath essences are '*proven* to relax', perhaps because an unconscious recollection of the *not proven* verdict gives a spurious air of scientific or legal authority to such claims. Readers who feel that they may be in error if they use *proved* rather than *proven* as the past participle of *prove* should, as always, take courage.

At the same time, it is important to note that when the word is used as an adjective – for example *'proven* facts', 'a *proven* track record' – *proven* is normal in British as well as American English. It should, however, be pronounced *proaven*, not *prooven*.

quantum leap   Not only is this now a rather tiresome cliché but its journalistic use as meaning 'a sudden and dramatic increase in scale or quantity' has always been mistaken. *Quantum leap*, or *quantum jump*, is a term from the world of sub-atomic particles, in which it means something like 'an abrupt transition from one *quantum* state to another', and should be left to people who are at home with such matters.

reason ... because   It is better to avoid the construction *The reason is because ...* because it is rather like saying *The reason is for the reason that ....* It is normally sufficient to say *The reason is that ....*

reason being, the   A speaker on a BBC natural history broadcast states that 'Numbers of this particular species have declined to worryingly low levels in recent years, and *the reason being is* that its habitat is being eroded by modern farming practices'. He might have said '... have declined ... in recent years, and the reason *is* ...' or '... have declined ... in recent years, *the reason being* that ...'. Instead, for some reason he decided to wear both belt and braces and produced '*the reason being is*'.

Why do people make this kind of mistake? It should go without saying that educated speakers don't say '*the reason being is*', but one suspects that 30 years ago uneducated speakers would not have done so either. As with so many other cases in this

103

book, might it be that modern educational methods have produced more rather than less insecurity about the way we use our language? Is it anxiety about some mistaken notion of 'correctness' that leads us into such absurdities as this one?

recrudescence   This word is quite often used as if it meant simply 'a return, a revival'. It is in fact a medical word meaning 'the breaking out again of a disease, the renewed inflammation of a wound', etc.; its Latin origin lies in words meaning 'making raw again'. In other words, *recrudescence* is rarely good news except for those hoping to benefit from the decease of a rich relative.

referendum   This was once a Latin gerundive meaning 'requiring to be referred'; its Latin plural is *referenda*. In modern English the only use of the word *referendum* is for the practice of referring a question to the vote of the entire electorate. Since the practice invariably involves only one question – for example, whether the United Kingdom should join the Single European Currency or whether Swiss women should be given the vote – the correct plural in English is *referendums*, not *referenda*. *Referenda* would mean 'matters requiring to be referred'.

See also AGENDA.

refute   To *refute* is to disprove by argument or by the production of evidence. It is not simply to *deny*, and police officers, football players and politicians who state that they *'refute'* allegations made against them are usually merely *denying*, *disputing* or *rejecting* them.

research   In British English this was normally stressed on the second syllable, whether used as a noun or a verb. Increasingly it is being pronounced in the American fashion with the stress on the first syllable, but there is no good reason for this.

resources   This is a perfectly good word that is, however, used with increasing frequency as a euphemism for 'money' or 'funding', especially by people who for one reason or another find it embarrassing to admit that what they are demand-ing is simply more cash, as in 'Our members simply cannot meet their health and safety responsibilities to the public without more *resources*'.

It is often found in contexts in which excuses are being sought for some failure of courage, efficiency or common sense, as in 'The local authority's failure to protect the children in its care from serious abuse is entirely down to lack of *resources*'.

The game is given away completely when the word is used as a singular noun, *resource* (that is, 'money') – as in 'what is needed is more *resource*' – or as a verb, *to resource* (that is, 'to fund'). Next time you hear some official spokesman talking about *resources*, ask yourself – or, if you can, ask him or her – exactly what he or she means by it.

Incidentally, the standard British English pronunciation is with the accent on the second syllable, but this seems to be giving way to the American pronunciation, with the accent on the first syllable. Once again, there seems to be no good reason for this.

restaurateur   The owner of a restaurant is a *restaurateur*, literally 'a restorer'. Traditionally he

106

promises to 'restore' our spirits and our physical well-being with his excellent food and wine. Neither in English nor in French does the word *restauranteur* properly exist.

restructuring   This is often nowadays used as a euphemism for the process by which costs are reduced in a commercial organisation by shedding staff, for example after a take-over or a merger.

See also DOWNSIZING.

reticent   Not long ago, the education correspondent of *The Times* stated that teachers were 'reticent to talk about violence in the classroom'. Since *reticent* means 'disinclined to speak freely; reserved', this could fairly be described as a tautology. *Reticent* does not mean simply 'reluctant', a word that would have served the education correspondent perfectly well in making her statement. This is one example out of many in which half-educated people use the wrong word in the belief that it is somehow smarter or more sophisticated than the plain old right one.

rites of passage   Rituals attending the passage from one stage of life to another, especially from youth to adulthood. *Right of passage* means something else entirely, for example the right of Russian naval vessels to pass through the Dardanelles Strait into the Mediterranean.

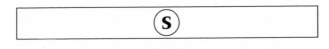
sacrilegious   This should be so spelt, and not as *sacreligious*. The latter misspelling probably results from the mistaken belief that the word has some etymological connection with *religion*. It does not.

safe haven   A *haven* is by definition a *safe* place for a ship to shelter in. An *unsafe haven* would be a contradiction in terms.

Sassenach   This is a Gaelic word for a 'Saxon', that is, an English-speaker, a category which, strictly speaking, should include speakers of Lowland Scots. Most Scots who use the word as a derogatory term for 'the English' are probably quite unaware that they may well be just as *Sassenach* as the people to the south of them.

schedule   The British English pronunciation is, or used to be, *shedule*. There is no good reason to replace it with the American pronunciation *skedule*.

109

secretary   There is a normal, educated pronunciation of this word, with an *r* at the beginning of the second syllable, and there is a special pronunciation favoured by trade union officials, politicians and many broadcasters, namely *secketary*.

show, showed, shown   The past tense of *show* is *showed*. ('The agent *showed* me the house'.) The past participle may be *shown* ('He has *shown* it to me') or *showed*, but *shown* is preferable. The passive form should always be *shown* ('It has been *shown*').

singular and plural   'For many people perceptions of greater community spirit *is* a positive advantage for residents.' (*State of the Countryside 2002*: Report from the Countryside Agency) 'Paul Robinson's purported description of my views on torture *are* a complete fabrication.' (Alan Dershowitz, letter in the *Spectator*, 1 May 2004)

It is quite remarkable these days how often, in speech and in print, we find cases such as the above, in which the number (singular or plural) of the verb is taken, not from the subject of the verb (in these cases, 'perceptions' and 'description'), but from the nearest noun (in these cases, 'spirit' and 'views').

What can be the reason for what is not merely ungrammatical English but actually *stupid* English? Is it that the writer or the speaker has such a short attention span that half way through the sentence he or she has forgotten how it started out? If so, the young woman who recently said on the BBC 'Today' programme, 'The diversity of these books *are* terrific' must have a very short attention span indeed, as must also the 'education spokesman' who, even more recently, referring to the theft of examination papers, declared, 'The security of the papers *are* questionable'.

And why is it that these strange lapses almost never occurred before c. 1990? Might it have something to do with the coming of age of a generation which went to primary school in the educationally 'progressive' late 1960s?

slither, sliver   A *sliver* is a slice, usually a very thin one, for example of *prosciutto*. The word is surprisingly often confused with *slither*, a verb meaning 'to move in a slippery fashion'.

111

sort of   See KIND OF.

sought-after   This phrase, meaning something like 'greatly in demand', has been noticed in estate agents' literature and elsewhere in the form *sort-after*. This is inexcusable ignorance.

stationary, stationery   The adjective meaning 'not moving' is spelt *stationary*. The noun meaning, broadly, 'writing materials' is spelt *stationery*.

still continues   Is any meaning lost if one says, simply, *continues*?

straitjacket, strait-laced   The *strait-* in these words means 'narrow, tight'. A *straitjacket* is designed to confine the arms of someone who might otherwise do damage to himself or others. Someone who is *strait-laced* is, in figurative terms, 'tightly corseted', hence 'prudish, puritanical'. Spellings with *straight-* are not acceptable.

stratum   The correct plural form is *strata*, which should be followed by a plural verb.

suffice to say   If one is going to use this rather old-fashioned expression one should get it right: *suffice it to say*, meaning 'let it be enough to say'. *Suffice to say* is ignorant and lazy.

supersede   This is the correct spelling. There is no such word as *supercede*.

syndrome   This is a word of Greek origin, meaning literally 'running together'. In its original medical sense it refers to a condition in which two or more symptoms appear together without any obvious causal link between them, as in Severe Acute Respiratory Syndrome, of which breathing difficulties are only one of the symptoms.

It may be quite properly used by extension into a wide range of characteristic combinations of behaviour, opinions etc., but it is important to retain the sense of two or more elements running together, rather than a single one.

talisman   The word derives from an Arabic via a Greek word, and the *-man* part of it has nothing to do with the species *Homo sapiens*. The plural is therefore *talismans*, not *talismen*.

tandem, in   People, animals or things *in tandem* are one in front of the other rather than side by side. (The expression has a rather jokey derivation from the Latin word *tandem* meaning 'at length'.) Thus horses may be harnessed *in tandem* or a couple may jointly pedal a *tandem* bicycle. The phrase does not mean simply 'jointly' or 'together'.

target   When using this word in a sense other than its literal one it is important to remember that a *target* may be aimed at, hit, missed, set at a greater or lesser distance or removed altogether, but not pursued, achieved, attained, kept to, obtained, increased or kept abreast of.

As a verb, meaning something like 'to designate as a *target*', it should be used with care, if at all.

task force   This is originally a military term for an *ad hoc* group of different types of unit brought together for a specific mission. Metaphorical use in non-military contexts may occasionally be justified, but a *task force* is not simply a 'working party' or a 'sub-committee' or any other body likely to produce minutes rather than practical results.

tenter-hooks, on   The phrase, meaning 'impatient, as if with nerves tautly strung', is so spelt and not as *on tender-hooks*.

throes of, in the   This is how the expression should be spelt. When seen in the form '*in the throws of*' it should be treated with ridicule and contempt.

transpire   This word once had (and still has) a technical meaning in the contexts of botany, biology and physics. Its present-day non-technical, figurative, meaning – 'to come to light, to emerge, to leak out, to become clear' – would at one time have been deplored, but is now entirely acceptable. It should not, however, be used as a synonym for 'happen' or 'occur'.

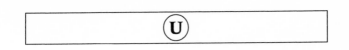

unique   Something is *unique* if it is the sole existing example of its type. The word derives from the Latin *unicus*, meaning 'one and only'. A thing can therefore be *quite unique* or perhaps even *almost unique* ('This 1932 limousine version is almost *unique*; only three were ever made'), but it is to misuse a valuable word to say *very unique, more unique, remarkably unique* etc.

venal, venial   These two Latinate words are easily confused but should not be.

Venal means 'corrupt, able to be bribed', as in 'the local police were thoroughly *venal*'.

Venial means 'forgivable, pardonable', as in '*venial* sins'.

vulnerable   The word should be pronounced with four syllables and with the *l* sounded, and not as *vunn'rable*.

who, whom   'The junior Civil Servant *whom* the Government has claimed is implicated in insider dealing has been allowed to return to work at the Office of Fair Trading.' (*The Times*, 1988, italics added)

As this example indicates, many people have a problem with whether to use *who* or *whom* as the relative pronoun in sentences of this kind. What seems to happen is that they see *whom* as the object of a verb, in this case 'has claimed', and fail to notice that this is subordinate to, in this case, 'The junior Civil Servant *who* ... is implicated in insider dealing ...'.

The matter becomes less confusing if we see phrases such as 'the Government has claimed' as parenthetic, and put imaginary brackets around them thus: 'The junior Civil Servant *who* (the Government has claimed) is implicated in insider dealing ...'.

The problem could be avoided altogether by

using the accusative plus infinitive – 'The junior Civil Servant *whom* the Government has claimed to be implicated in insider dealing ...' – but this may well be thought to be too formal for current usage.

yew and non-yew   One way of riling an enemy to the point where he loses his head and starts making mistakes is deliberately and continually to mispronounce his name. In the Second World War there was not a lot that Winston Churchill could do with the name Hitler, but he made a point of mispronouncing the name of Hitler's party, the 'Naaazzis'.

Friends and allies are a different matter, and given the desirability of being on good terms with the current Russian President, it is surprising that the Foreign Office has apparently made no effort to brief the Prime Minister or the Foreign Secretary on getting his name right, surely a matter of elementary diplomatic courtesy. Whatever the most correct Russian pronunciation of the name 'Putin' may be, it is certainly not 'Pew-tin', but that is how it sounds on the lips of Britain's leading statesmen, not to mention some BBC correspondents and others who ought to know better.

Incidentally, one consequence of John Birt's internal market 'reforms' at the BBC was that the renowned Pronunciation Unit was compelled to charge other BBC departments for its services. For departmental managers with tight budgets this must have been recognised as one of the easier ways of making small economies, but it seems a great pity, and is clearly having an effect.

George Orwell, 'Politics and the English Language', 1946

Most people who bother with the matter at all would admit that the English language is in a bad way, but it is generally assumed that we cannot by conscious action do anything about it. Our civilization is decadent and our language – so the argument runs – must inevitably share in the general collapse. It follows that any struggle against the abuse of language is a sentimental archaism, like preferring candles to electric light or hansom cabs to aeroplanes. Underneath this lies the half-conscious belief that language is a natural growth and not an instrument which we shape for our own purposes.

Now, it is clear that the decline of a language must ultimately have political and economic causes: it is not due simply to the bad influence of this or that individual writer. But an effect can become a cause, reinforcing the original cause and producing the same effect in an intensified form, and so on indefinitely. A man may take to drink because he feels himself to be a failure, and then fail all the more completely because he drinks. It is rather the same thing that is happening to the English language. It becomes ugly and inaccurate because our thoughts are foolish, but the slovenliness of our language makes it easier for us to have foolish thoughts. The point is that the process is reversible. Modern English, especially written English, is full of bad habits which spread by imitation and which can be avoided if one is willing to take the necessary trouble. If one gets rid of these habits one can think more clearly, and to think clearly is a necessary first step towards political regeneration: so that the fight against bad English is not frivolous and is not the exclusive concern of professional writers. I will come back to this presently, and I hope that by that time the meaning of what I have said here will have become clearer. Meanwhile, here are five specimens of the English language as it is now habitually written.

These five passages have not been picked out because they are especially bad – I could have quoted far worse if I had chosen – but because they illustrate various of the mental vices from which we now suffer. They are a little below the average, but are fairly representative examples. I number them so that I can refer back to them when necessary:

1. I am not, indeed, sure whether it is not true to say that the Milton who once seemed not unlike a seventeenth-century Shelley had not become, out of an experience ever more bitter in each year, more alien [*sic*] to the founder of that Jesuit sect which nothing could induce him to tolerate.

   Professor Harold Laski (Essay in
   Freedom of Expression)

2. Above all, we cannot play ducks and drakes with a native battery of idioms which prescribes egregious collocations of vocables as the Basic *put up with* for *tolerate*, or *put at a loss* for *bewilder*.

   Professor Lancelot Hogben (*Interglossa*)

3. On the one side we have the free personality: by definition it is not neurotic, for it has neither conflict nor dream. Its desires, such as they are, are transparent, for they are just what institutional approval keeps in the forefront of

consciousness; another institutional pattern would alter their number and intensity; there is little in them that is natural, irreducible, or culturally dangerous. But *on the other side*, the social bond itself is nothing but the mutual reflection of these self-secure integrities. Recall the definition of love. Is not this the very picture of a small academic? Where is there a place in this hall of mirrors for either personality or fraternity?

Essay on psychology in *Politics* (New York)

4. All the 'best people' from the gentlemen's clubs, and all the frantic fascist captains, united in common hatred of Socialism and bestial horror at the rising tide of the mass revolutionary movement, have turned to acts of provocation, to foul incendiarism, to medieval legends of poisoned wells, to legalize their own destruction of proletarian organizations, and rouse the agitated petty-bourgeoisie to chauvinistic fervour on behalf of the fight against the revolutionary way out of the crisis.

Communist pamphlet

5. If a new spirit is to be infused into this old country, there is one thorny and contentious reform which must be tackled, and that is the humanization and galvanization of the B.B.C. Timidity here will bespeak canker and atrophy of the soul. The heart of Britain may be sound and of strong beat, for instance, but the British lion's roar at present is like that of Bottom in Shakespeare's *Midsummer Night's Dream* – as gentle as any sucking dove. A virile new Britain cannot continue indefinitely to be traduced in the eyes, or rather ears, of the world by the effete languors of Langham Place, brazenly masquerading as 'standard English'. When the Voice of Britain is heard at nine o'clock, better far and infinitely less ludicrous to hear aitches honestly dropped than the present priggish, inflated, inhibited, school-ma'amish arch braying of blameless bashful mewing maidens!

Letter in *Tribune*

Each of these passages has faults of its own, but, quite apart from avoidable ugliness, two qualities are common to all of them. The first is staleness of imagery; the other is lack of precision. The writer either has a meaning and cannot express it, or he inadvertently says something else, or he is almost indifferent as to whether his words mean anything or not. This mixture of vagueness and sheer incompetence is the most marked characteristic of modern English prose, and especially of any kind of political writing. As soon as certain topics are raised, the concrete melts into the abstract and no one seems able to think of turns of speech that are not hackneyed: prose consists less and less of *words* chosen for the sake of their meaning, and more and more of *phrases* tacked together like the sections of a prefabricated hen-house. I list below, with notes and examples, various of the tricks by means of which the work of prose construction is habitually dodged:

Dying metaphors. A newly invented metaphor assists thought by evoking a visual image, while on the other hand a metaphor which is technically 'dead' (e.g. *iron resolution*) has in effect reverted to being an ordinary word and can generally be used without loss of vividness. But in between these two

132

classes there is a huge dump of worn-out metaphors which have lost all evocative power and are merely used because they save people the trouble of inventing phrases for themselves. Examples are: *Ring the changes on, take up the cudgels for, toe the line, ride roughshod over, stand shoulder to shoulder with, play into the hands of, no axe to grind, grist to the mill, fishing in troubled waters, rift within the lute, on the order of the day, Achilles' heel, swan song, hotbed.* Many of these are used without knowledge of their meaning (what is a 'rift', for instance?), and incompatible metaphors are frequently mixed, a sure sign that the writer is not interested in what he is saying. Some metaphors now current have been twisted out of their original meaning without those who use them even being aware of the fact. For example, *toe the line* is sometimes written as *tow the line*. Another example is *the hammer and the anvil*, now always used with the implication that the anvil gets the worst of it. In real life it is always the anvil that breaks the hammer, never the other way about: a writer who stopped to think what he was saying would avoid perverting the original phrase.

Operators or *verbal false limbs*. These save the trouble of picking out appropriate verbs and nouns, and at the same time pad each sentence with extra syllables which give it an appearance of symmetry. Characteristic phrases are *render inoperative, militate against, prove unacceptable, make contact with, be subject to, give rise to, give grounds for, have the effect of, play a leading part (role) in, make itself felt, take effect, exhibit a tendency to, serve the purpose of,* etc., etc. The keynote is the elimination of simple verbs. Instead of being a single word, such as *break, stop, spoil, mend, kill,* a verb becomes a *phrase,* made up of a noun or adjective tacked on to some general-purpose verb such as *prove, serve, form, play, render.* In addition, the passive voice is wherever possible used in preference to the active, and noun constructions are used instead of gerunds (*by examination of* instead of *by examining*). The range of verbs is further cut down by means of the *-ize* and *de-* formations, and banal statements are given an appearance of profundity by means of the *not un-* formation. Simple conjunctions and prepositions are replaced by such phrases as *with respect to, having regard to, the fact that, by dint of, in view of, in the* *interests of, on the hypothesis that*; and the ends of sentences are saved from anticlimax by such resounding commonplaces as *greatly to be desired, cannot be left out of account, a development to be expected in the near future, deserving of serious consideration, brought to a satisfactory conclusion,* and so on and so forth.

Pretentious diction. Words like *phenomenon, element, individual* (as noun), *objective, categorical, effective, virtual, basic, primary, promote, constitute, exhibit, exploit, utilize, eliminate, liquidate,* are used to dress up simple statements and give an air of scientific impartiality to biased judgements. Adjectives like *epoch-making, epic, historic, unforgettable, triumphant, age-old, inevitable, inexorable, veritable,* are used to dignify the sordid processes of international politics, while writing that aims at glorifying war usually takes on an archaic colour, its characteristic words being: *realm, throne, chariot, mailed fist, trident, sword, shield, buckler, banner, jackboot, clarion.* Foreign words and expressions such as *cul de sac, ancien régime, deus ex machina, mutatis mutandis, status quo, Gleichschaltung, Weltanschauung,* are used to give an air of culture and elegance. Except for the useful abbreviations *i.e.*, *e.g.* and *etc.*, there is no real need for any of the hundreds of foreign phrases now current in English. Bad writers, and especially scientific, political and sociological writers, are nearly always haunted by the notion that Latin or Greek words are grander than Saxon ones, and unnecessary words like *expedite, ameliorate, predict, extraneous, deracinated, clandestine, sub-aqueous* and hundreds of others constantly gain ground from their Anglo-Saxon opposite numbers.* The jargon peculiar to Marxist writing (*hyena, hangman, cannibal, petty bourgeois, these gentry, lackey, flunkey, mad dog, White Guard,* etc.) consists largely of words and phrases translated from Russian, German or French; but the normal way of coining a new word is to use a Latin or Greek root with the appropriate affix and, where necessary, the *-ize* formation.

---

* An interesting illustration of this is the way in which the English flower names which were in use till very recently are being ousted by Greek ones, *snapdragon* becoming *antirrhinum, forget-me-not* becoming *myosotis,* etc. It is hard to see any practical reason for this change of fashion: it is probably due to an instinctive turning-away from the more homely word and a vague feeling that the Greek word is scientific.

It is often easier to make up words of this kind (*deregionalize, impermissible, extramarital, non-fragmentary* and so forth) than to think up the English words that will cover one's meaning. The result, in general, is an increase in slovenliness and vagueness.

Meaningless words. In certain kinds of writing, particularly in art criticism and literary criticism, it is normal to come across long passages which are almost completely lacking in meaning.* Words like *romantic, plastic, values, human, dead, sentimental, natural, vitality,* as used in art criticism, are strictly meaningless, in the sense that they not only do not point to any discoverable object, but are hardly even expected to do so by the reader. When one critic writes, 'The outstanding feature of Mr X's

---

* Example: 'Comfort's catholicity of perception and image, strangely Whitmanesque in range, almost the exact opposite in aesthetic compulsion, continues to evoke that trembling atmospheric accumulative hinting at a cruel, an inexorably serene timelessness ... Wrey Gardiner scores by aiming at simple bullseyes with precision. Only they are not so simple, and through this contented sadness runs more than the surface bitter-sweet of resignation. (*Poetry Quarterly.*)

work is its living quality', while another writes, 'The immediately striking thing about Mr X's work is its peculiar deadness', the reader accepts this as a simple difference of opinion. If words like *black* and *white* were involved, instead of the jargon words *dead* and *living*, he would see at once that language was being used in an improper way. Many political words are similarly abused. The word *Fascism* has now no meaning except in so far as it signifies 'something not desirable'. The words *democracy*, *socialism, freedom, patriotic, realistic, justice*, have each of them several different meanings which cannot be reconciled with one another. In the case of a word like *democracy*, not only is there no agreed definition, but the attempt to make one is resisted from all sides. It is almost universally felt that when we call a country democratic we are praising it: consequently the defenders of every kind of régime claim that it is a democracy, and fear that they might have to stop using the word if it were tied down to any one meaning. Words of this kind are often used in a consciously dishonest way. That is, the person who uses them has his own private definition, but allows his hearer to think he means something quite different. Statements like *Marshal Pétain was a true patriot, The Soviet press is the freest in the world, The Catholic Church is opposed to persecution,* are almost always made with intent to deceive. Other words used in variable meanings, in most cases more or less dishonestly, are: *class, totalitarian, science, progressive, reactionary, bourgeois, equality.*

Now that I have made this catalogue of swindles and perversions, let me give another example of the kind of writing that they lead to. This time it must of its nature be an imaginary one. I am going to translate a passage of good English into modern English of the worst sort. Here is a well-known verse from *Ecclesiastes*:

> I returned, and saw under the sun, that the race is not to the swift, nor the battle to the strong, neither yet bread to the wise, nor yet riches to men of understanding, nor yet favour to men of skill; but time and chance happeneth to them all.

Here it is in modern English:

> Objective consideration of contemporary phenomena compels the conclusion that success or failure in competitive activities exhibits no tendency to be commensurate with innate capacity, but that a considerable element of the unpredictable must invariably be taken into account.

This is a parody, but not a very gross one. Exhibit 3, above, for instance, contains several patches of the same kind of English. It will be seen that I have not made a full translation. The beginning and ending of the sentence follow the original meaning fairly closely, but in the middle the concrete illustrations – race, battle, bread – dissolve into the vague phrase 'success or failure in competitive activities'. This had to be so, because no modern writer of the kind I am discussing – no one capable of using phrases like 'objective consideration of contemporary phenomena' – would ever tabulate his thoughts in that precise and detailed way. The whole tendency of modern prose is away from concreteness. Now analyse these two sentences a little more closely. The first contains 49 words but only 60 syllables, and all its words are those of everyday life. The second contains 38 words of 90 syllables: 18 of its words are from Latin roots, and one from Greek. The first sentence contains six vivid images, and only one phrase ('time and chance') that could be called vague. The second contains not a single fresh, arresting phrase, and in spite of its 90 syllables it gives only a shortened version of the meaning contained in the first. Yet without a doubt it is the second kind of sentence that is gaining ground in modern English. I do not want to exaggerate. This kind of writing is not yet universal, and outcrops of simplicity will occur here and there in the worst-written page. Still, if you or I were told to write a few lines on the uncertainty of human fortunes, we should probably come much nearer to my imaginary sentence than to the one from *Ecclesiastes*.

As I have tried to show, modern writing at its worst does not consist in picking out words for the sake of their meaning and inventing images in order to make the meaning clearer. It consists in gumming together long strips of words which have already been set in order by someone else, and making the results presentable by sheer humbug. The attraction of this way of writing is that it is easy. It is easier – even quicker, once you have the habit – to say *In my opinion it is not an unjustifiable assumption that* than to say *I think*. If you use ready-made phrases, you not only don't have to hunt about for the words; you also don't have to bother with the rhythms of your sentences since these phrases are generally so arranged as to be more or less euphonious. When you are composing in a hurry – when you are dictating to a stenographer, for instance, or making a public speech – it is natural to fall into a pretentious, latinized style. Tags like *a consideration which we should do well to bear in mind* or *a conclusion to which all of us would readily assent* will save many a sentence from coming down with a bump. By using stale metaphors, similes and idioms, you save much mental effort, at the cost of leaving your meaning vague, not only for your reader but for yourself. This is the significance of mixed metaphors. The sole aim of a metaphor is to call up a visual image. When these images clash – as in *The Fascist octopus has sung its swan song, the jackboot is thrown into the melting pot* – it can be taken as certain that the writer is not seeing a mental image of the objects he is naming; in other words he is not really thinking. Look again at the examples I gave at the beginning of this essay. Professor Laski (1) uses five negatives in 53 words. One of these is superfluous, making nonsense of the whole passage, and in addition there is the slip *alien* for akin, making further nonsense, and several avoidable pieces of clumsiness which increase the general vagueness. Professor Hogben (2) plays ducks and drakes with a battery which is able to write prescriptions, and, while disapproving of the everyday phrase *put up with*, is unwilling to look *egregious* up in the dictionary and see what it means. (3), if one takes an uncharitable attitude towards it, is simply meaningless: probably one could work out its intended meaning by reading the whole of the article in which it occurs. In (4), the writer knows more or less what he wants to say, but an accumulation of stale phrases chokes him like tea-leaves blocking a sink. In (5), words and meaning have almost parted company. People who write in this manner usually have a general emotional meaning – they dislike one thing and want to express

143

solidarity with another – but they are not interested in the detail of what they are saying. A scrupulous writer, in every sentence that he writes, will ask himself at least four questions, thus: What am I trying to say? What words will express it? What image or idiom will make it clearer? Is this image fresh enough to have an effect? And he will probably ask himself two more: Could I put it more shortly? Have I said anything that is avoidably ugly? But you are not obliged to go to all this trouble. You can shirk it by simply throwing your mind open and letting the ready-made phrases come crowding in. They will construct your sentences for you – even think your thoughts for you, to a certain extent – and at need they will perform the important service of partially conceal-ing your meaning even from yourself. It is at this point that the special connection between politics and the debasement of language becomes clear.

In our time it is broadly true that political writing is bad writing. Where it is not true, it will generally be found that the writer is some kind of rebel, expressing his private opinions and not a 'party line'. Orthodoxy, of whatever colour, seems to demand a lifeless, imitative style. The political dialects to be found in pamphlets, leading articles, manifestoes, White Papers and the speeches of Under-Secretaries do, of course, vary from party to party, but they are all alike in that one almost never finds in them a fresh, vivid, home-made turn of speech. When one watches some tired hack on the platform mechanically repeating the familiar phrases – *bestial atrocities, iron heel, blood-stained tyranny, free peoples of the world, stand shoulder to shoulder* – one often has a curious feeling that one is not watching a live human being but some kind of dummy: a feeling which suddenly becomes stronger at moments when the light catches the speaker's spectacles and turns them into blank discs which seem to have no eyes behind them. And this is not altogether fanciful. A speaker who uses that kind of phraseology has gone some distance towards turning himself into a machine. The appropriate noises are coming out of his larynx, but his brain is not involved as it would be if he were choosing his words for himself. If the speech he is making is one that he is accustomed to make over and over again, he may be almost unconscious of what he is saying, as one is when one utters the responses in church. And this reduced state of consciousness, if not indispensable, is at any rate favourable to political conformity.

In our time, political speech and writing are largely the defence of the indefensible. Things like the continuance of British rule in India, the Russian purges and deportations, the dropping of the atom bombs on Japan, can indeed be defended, but only by arguments which are too brutal for most people to face, and which do not square with the professed aims of political parties. Thus political language has to consist largely of euphemism, question-begging and sheer cloudy vagueness. Defenceless villages are bombarded from the air, the inhabitants driven out into the countryside, the cattle machine-gunned, the huts set on fire with incendiary bullets: this is called *pacification*. Millions of peasants are robbed of their farms and sent trudging along the roads with no more than they can carry: this is called *transfer of population* or *rectification of frontiers*. People are imprisoned for years without trial, or shot in the back of the neck or sent to die of scurvy in Arctic lumber camps: this is called *elimination of unreliable elements.* Such phraseology is needed if one wants to name things without calling up mental pictures of them. Consider for instance some comfortable English professor defending Russian totalitarianism. He cannot say outright, 'I believe in killing off your opponents when you can get good results by doing so.' Probably, therefore, he will say something like this:

> While freely conceding that the Soviet régime exhibits certain features which the humanitarian may be inclined to deplore, we must, I think, agree that a certain curtailment of the right to political opposition is an unavoidable concomitant of transitional periods, and that the rigours which the Russian people have been called upon to undergo have been amply justified in the sphere of concrete achievement.

The inflated style is itself a kind of euphemism. A mass of Latin words falls upon the facts like soft snow, blurring the outlines and covering up all the details. The great enemy of clear language is insincerity. When there is a gap between one's real and one's declared aims, one turns as it were instinctively to long words and exhausted idioms, like a cuttlefish squirting out ink. In our age there is no such thing as 'keeping out of politics'. All issues are political issues, and politics itself is a mass of lies, evasions, folly, hatred and schizophrenia. When the general atmosphere is bad, language must suffer. I should expect to find – this is a guess which I have not sufficient knowledge to verify – that the German, Russian and Italian languages have all deteriorated in the last ten or fifteen years, as a result of dictatorship.

But if thought corrupts language, language can also corrupt thought. A bad usage can spread by tradition and imitation even among people who should and do know better. The debased language that I have been discussing is in some ways very convenient. Phrases like *a not unjustifiable assumption, leaves much to be desired, would serve no good purpose, a consideration which we should do well to bear in mind,* are a continuous temptation, a packet of aspirins always at one's elbow. Look back through this essay, and for certain you will find that I have again and again committed the very faults I am

148

protesting against. By this morning's post I have received a pamphlet dealing with conditions in Germany. The author tells me that he 'felt impelled' to write it. I open it at random, and here is almost the first sentence that I see: '[The Allies] have an opportunity not only of achieving a radical transformation of Germany's social and political structure in such a way as to avoid a nationalistic reaction in Germany itself, but at the same time of laying the foundations of a co-operative and unified Europe.' You see, he 'feels impelled' to write – feels, presumably, that he has something new to say – and yet his words, like cavalry horses answering the bugle, group themselves automatically into the familiar dreary pattern. This invasion of one's mind by ready-made phrases (*lay the foundations, achieve a radical transformation*) can only be prevented if one is constantly on guard against them, and every such phrase anaesthetizes a portion of one's brain.

I said earlier that the decadence of our language is probably curable. Those who deny this would argue, if they produced an argument at all, that language merely reflects existing social conditions, and that we cannot influence its development by any direct tinkering with words and constructions. So far as the general tone or spirit of a language goes, this may be true, but it is not true in detail. Silly words and expressions have often disappeared, not through any evolutionary process but owing to the conscious action of a minority. Two recent examples were *explore every avenue* and *leave no stone unturned*, which were killed by the jeers of a few journalists. There is a long list of fly-blown metaphors which could similarly be got rid of if enough people would interest themselves in the job; and it should also be possible to laugh the *not un-* formation out of existence,* to reduce the amount of Latin and Greek in the average sentence, to drive out foreign phrases and strayed scientific words, and, in general, to make pretentiousness unfashionable. But all these are minor points. The defence of the English language implies more than this, and perhaps it is best to start by saying what it does *not* imply.

* One can cure oneself of the *not un-* formation by memorizing this sentence: *A not unblack dog was chasing a not unsmall rabbit across a not ungreen field.*

To begin with it has nothing to do with archaism, with the salvaging of obsolete words and turns of speech, or with the setting up of a 'standard English' which must never be departed from. On the contrary, it is especially concerned with the scrapping of every word or idiom which has outworn its usefulness. It has nothing to do with correct grammar and syntax, which are of no importance so long as one makes one's meaning clear, or with the avoidance of Americanisms, or with having what is called a 'good prose style'. On the other hand it is not concerned with fake simplicity and the attempt to make written English colloquial. Nor does it even imply in every case preferring the Saxon word to the Latin one, though it does imply using the fewest and shortest words that will cover one's meaning. What is above all needed is to let the meaning choose the word, and not the other way about. In prose, the worst thing you can do with words is surrender to them. When you think of a concrete object, you think word-lessly, and then, if you want to describe the thing you have been visualizing, you probably hunt about till you find the exact words that seem to fit it.

When you think of something abstract you are more inclined to use words from the start, and unless you make a conscious effort to prevent it, the existing dialect will come rushing in and do the job for you, at the expense of blurring or even changing your meaning. Probably it is better to put off using words as long as possible and get one's meaning as clear as one can through pictures and sensations. Afterwards one can choose – not simply *accept* – the phrases that will best cover the meaning, and then switch round and decide what impression one's words are likely to make on another person. This last effort of the mind cuts out all stale or mixed images, all prefabricated phrases, needless repetitions, and humbug and vagueness generally. But one can often be in doubt about the effect of a word or a phrase, and one needs rules that one can rely on when instinct fails. I think the following rules will cover most cases:

  i. Never use a metaphor, simile or other figure of speech which you are used to seeing in print.
 ii. Never use a long word where a short one will do.

iii. If it is possible to cut a word out, always cut it out.

iv. Never use the passive where you can use the active.

v. Never use a foreign phrase, a scientific word or a jargon word if you can think of an everyday English equivalent.

vi. Break any of these rules sooner than say anything outright barbarous.

These rules sound elementary, and so they are, but they demand a deep change of attitude in anyone who has grown used to writing in the style now fashionable. One could keep all of them and still write bad English, but one could not write the kind of stuff that I quoted in those five specimens at the beginning of this article.

I have not here been considering the literary use of language, but merely language as an instrument for expressing and not for concealing or preventing thought. Stuart Chase and others have come near to claiming that all abstract words are meaningless, and have used this as a pretext for advocating a kind of political quietism. Since you don't know what Fascism is, how can you struggle against Fascism? One need not swallow such absurdities as this, but one ought to recognize that the present political chaos is connected with the decay of language, and that one can probably bring about some improvement by starting at the verbal end. If you simplify your English, you are freed from the worst follies of orthodoxy. You cannot speak any of the necessary dialects, and when you make a stupid remark its stupidity will be obvious, even to yourself. Political language – and with variations this is true of all political parties, from Conservatives to Anarchists – is designed to make lies sound truthful and murder respectable, and to give an appearance of solidity to pure wind. One cannot change this all in a moment, but one can at least change one's own habits, and from time to time one can even, if one jeers loudly enough, send some worn-out and useless phrase – some *jackboot*, *Achilles' heel*, *hotbed*, *melting pot*, *acid test*, *veritable inferno*, or other lump of verbal refuse – into the dustbin where it belongs.